TAKE THE PLACE'S
FINGERPRINT.
Forget words such as
resource, site, customers
and public. Abstractions
lead us astray.
Think and talk about
PLACES AND
PEOPLE.

Get to know your
GHOSTS.
The hidden and unseen
STORIES
AND
LEGENDS
are as important
as the visible.

**GROUND
YOURSELF,**
attachment is the
first step to
CHANGING
THE WORLD.

Don't fossilise places.
HISTORY
is a continuing process,
not just the past.
Celebrate time, place
and the seasons with
FEASTS AND
FESTIVALS.

Work for
LOCA
IDENTIT
OPPOSE
MONOCULT
in our fields, pa
gardens and buildings.
**RESIST
FORMULAIC
DESIGNS**
and automatic ordering
from pattern books
*which homogenise
and deplete.*

Our **imagination** needs
DIVERSITY
and variegation.
WE NEED
STANDARDS,
not
standardisation.

JETTISON YOUR CAR
whenever you can and go
by public transport.
PLACES ARE FOR
PEOPLE
AND
NATURE.
*Cars detach us from places
and unwittingly cause
their destruction.*

WISDOM.
*Itinerant expertise needs to
meet with aboriginal,
place-based knowledge so
that we can make the*
BEST OF BOTH
WORLDS.

THE **LAND** IS
SACRED
in many cultures. Why
have we put a protective
noose around the
SPECTACULAR
AND THE
SPECIAL
and left the rest?
*All of our surroundings are
important to someone.*

Buy things that are
**LOCALLY
DISTINCTIVE**
AND
LOCALLY
MADE
*– such as food and souvenirs.
Resist the things that can be
found anywhere.*

JOURNEYS THROUGH

ENGLAND IN PARTICULAR:

On Foot

JOURNEYS THROUGH

ENGLAND IN PARTICULAR:

On Foot

SUE CLIFFORD & ANGELA KING

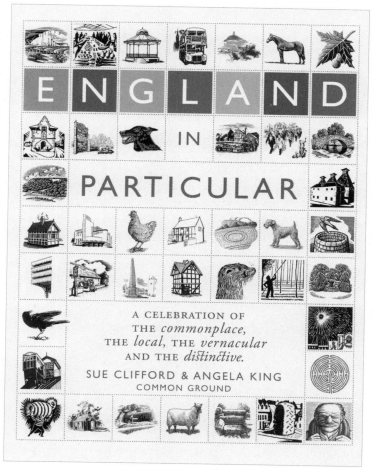

ENGLAND IN PARTICULAR

A CELEBRATION OF
THE *commonplace*,
THE *local*, THE *vernacular*
AND THE *distinctive*.

SUE CLIFFORD & ANGELA KING
COMMON GROUND

Acclaim for *England in Particular*

'A living portrait of England here and now, with all the narrative and mystery of the past attached ... The book is gracefully written, phenomenally knowledgeable, and simply exhilarating, speaking as it does of the extraordinary things that are all around us, if we are only prepared to open our eyes to them.'   FAY WELDON

'There is an impressive synoptic quality to the essays, which are given further unity by the lyrical character of the prose, by the rich, warm, humorous, celebratory tone throughout and the lightness of the authors' touch with the facts. Yet this is also a wonderfully scholarly book ... The book is an absolute delight for dippers, but there is a serious and unifying philosophy underpinning it ... The abiding satisfaction of this superb book is to make us aware, perhaps for the first time, of something as wonderful and simple as a hollow way, and to allow us to appreciate it as both rural commonplace and national treasure all at once.'

MARK COCKER, *Guardian*

'This book is, if you like, a sermon on the art of cherishing, and also on the art of noticing. It is not a question of clinging to the past; rather of accepting that the past is what gives us definition and existence.'

SIMON BARNES, *The Times*
England in Particular was No 4 in *The Times* Top Ten Books of 2006.

'It should be added to Dorothy Hartley's similarly inspiring book published in 1954 called *Food in England*, to Richard Mabey's *Flora Britannica* and the equally wonderful *Birds Britannica*, to make a quartet of books guaranteed to receive enthusiasm for our island home. This book is the antidote to surfing the net. Spend an afternoon in its company and the view from your window will never be the same again.'

SIMONE SEKERS, *Blackmore Vale Magazine*

'This book is not a description but a manifesto, not a catalogue of charms but an urge to action and to a new way of seeing England. It is a ragbag of riches dragged up from all over England into which you can plunge your hand, elbow- and shoulder-deep. Here, the authors say over and over again, are the valuable things which you had scarcely noticed were valuable before. As a result, it is a deeply optimistic book. Gravestones matter as much as graffiti, grassy triangles and granite: all take their place as part of the language that the English use to know who they are.'

ADAM NICOLSON, *Evening Standard*

'An entrancing green alphabet ... "The land is our most elaborate story board," say Sue Clifford and Angela King as they demonstrate this truth in seemingly countless small essays, each one a brief masterpiece of combined natural and social history ... this is a book for all English seasons and for every English mile.'

RONALD BLYTHE

'This wise and witty and broad-shouldered celebration is the triumphant fruition of their work with Common Ground.'

RICHARD MABEY

'Thank heavens for this book. *England in Particular* does everything that the ideal grandmother would, with equal charm and perhaps an even greater depth of accuracy and information. It should become part of every well-organised family.'

CLIVE ASLET, *Country Life*

'As vital as it is joyous, and as timely as it is inspired ... It should join Shakespeare and the Bible as a "must have" on any English man or woman's desert island.'

HUGH FEARNLEY-WHITTINGSTALL

'It should be at every curious Englishman's bedside.'

ALAN TITCHMARSH

CONTENTS

CELEBRATING LOCAL DISTINCTIVENESS

This book is about the extraordinary richness of our everyday surroundings; the landscapes, buildings, people and wildlife that give meaning to the places we know.

It is about the commonplace; for us to value it, a creature does not have to be endangered, a building does not have to be monumental, a prospect does not have to be breathtaking. A place may not even be 'ours' for us to feel attached to it. We just need to know something of it; it has to mean something to us.

Everywhere is somewhere. What makes each place unique is the conspiracy of nature and culture; the accumulation of story upon history upon natural history.

At Common Ground we forged the idea of *local distinctiveness* to embody this concept. It is a dynamic thing, constantly evolving as places change – it is not about preserving the status quo, creating a frozen moment – and it includes the invisible as well as the visible: symbols, festivals and legends stand alongside hedgerows, hills and houses.

We have focused on aspects of locality – archaeology, architecture, landscape, language, food, folklore, events, engineering – that interact with one another at the level of the street, the neighbourhood, the parish.

Why England? Because we know it best. But we offer a way of looking that has universal potential, though it is best done on an intimate scale.

Why A to Z? The alphabet helps us to break some conventions; it liberates us from classifying things, from following history as an arrow through time, from organising hierarchies. It shuffles and juxtaposes in ways that surprise. This can change what we see, make things we take for granted seem new to us; it may encourage us into action. We hope this book helps you to look at your own place, to see it through new eyes, to cherish it and to take it into your own hands.

SUE CLIFFORD & ANGELA KING

Notes

England in Particular: a celebration of the commonplace, local, the vernacular and the distinctive. Sue Clifford & Angela King. Hodder & Stoughton 2006. Saltyard 2013. The original book is over 500 pages long with nearly 600 essays. It has a substantial preliminary essay, a fuller bibliography and an index.

The essays and illustrations in this new series are all taken from this book.

Journeys Through England in Particular: On Foot

Journeys Through England in Particular: Coasting

The English Counties

The Historic Counties are used. We have done our best to follow the bounds laid down a thousand years ago or more, helped by old maps and gazetteers, especially that online, produced by the Association of British Counties. Inevitably we have found it difficult and admit to inconsistencies especially in and around the cities.

'What do you consider the largest map that would be really useful?'

'About six inches to the mile.'

'Only six inches!' exclaimed Mein Herr. 'We very soon got to six yards to the mile. Then we tried a hundred yards to the mile. And then came the grandest idea of all! We actually made a map of the country, on the scale of a mile to the mile!'

'Have you used it much?' I enquired.

'It has never been spread out yet,' said Mein Herr: 'the farmers objected: they said it would cover the whole country, and shut out the sunlight! So we now use the country itself, as its own map, and I assure you it does nearly as well.'

LEWIS CARROLL, from *Sylvie and Bruno Concluded*

ALLEYS

Between buildings or hedge and fence, the narrow walkway, wide enough for a person but not much more, is a reminder of the importance of permeability in the old parts of city, town and village.

Some alleys are public routes, others more private, as in Arab towns. Many travel under or through buildings (some as 'entries' through to the back yards of terraced houses); slopes may be negotiated by steps. They follow memories of old ownerships and rights of way that are now intimate short cuts for the cognoscenti. Such is their intricacy and particularity that many carry local names.

'In Hull (where my parents come from) they say ten foot – these connect the front of the house to your own back garden, between one house and the next. Great places for playing ball,' Rosie Cross says. She goes on: *'Here in Teesdale we use the word wynd (and it is in many addresses), pronounced "weend" – this is an alley or windy narrow lane.'*

Marylebone Passage at the back of Oxford Street, London survived the relentless pressure of building and is a relic of a well-used footpath all the way from St Giles in the Fields in Covent Garden to St Mary's. More intimate courts, yards and passages may have survived but lost their

sky to the upper floors of buildings, as often happens in York – Coffee Yard, St Crux Passage to Whip-ma-whop-ma-gate and ways to and from The Shambles.

In Dorset, as Chris Slade observes, *'a drong is a narrow way between hedges, fences or walls. It appears on maps (and in the OED) as I have spelt it, but I have only heard it pronounced "drawn".'* This lengthened sound, with a swallowed end, is how it would rhyme in William Barnes's nineteenth-century dialect poem 'The Turnstile':

Bakehouse Yard, Haggersgate, Whitby, Yorkshire.

> *On Steän-cliff road, within the drong,*
> *Up where, as v'ok do pass along,*
> *The turnen stile, a païnted white,*
> *Do sheen by day an' show by night.*

While snicket sometimes appears in dictionaries as a northern dialect word describing a passage between buildings or fences, other well-used local terms are more elusive. '*Twitchel is used in Derbyshire to mean a narrow footpath between houses or running alongside fields,*' says Daphne Anson of Hunstanton, Norfolk. '*It is of a width that can carry two people, say, side by side; could possibly give room for a horse, although it is not officially a bridle path; and certainly nowadays can accommodate a bicycle. It is open to everyone. Sometimes it is defined by hedges, though in places these may be replaced by a fence.*'

Around Nottingham, heading in different directions out of the city, you might find twitchel, ginnel or jitty used, a reminder of the simmering of cultures here during the so-called Dark Ages. Further north you will find more commonly gennel or gunnal, all with a hard 'g'. A passage between walls in Beverley, east Yorkshire is a racket.

Richard Barton says: '*I was brought up in Sussex, and the name we used was twitten for an alleyway behind some shops. I was in Hamburg, Germany some years ago and the name for a similar alleyway or small street is Twiet in Plattdeutsch, or Low German, which is still spoken in that part of Germany. Twiet rhymes with street.*' The oldest area of Brighton, Sussex, bordered by North, East and West streets, is called the Lanes, which is full of twittens. The narrow cobbled alleys are bordered by mainly eighteenth- and nineteenth-century buildings on a medieval street pattern, having been rebuilt more than once after ravages by the French and the sea (South Street has been found under beach shingle). These are no longer back alleys: tourists and locals linger in the antiques and clothes shops, cafés and pubs.

On the Isle of Portland, Dorset, an ope is a narrow passage between houses or walls that opens towards the sea. Margaret Somerville explains: 'We have come up with seven "openings to the sea", lanes particular to Chiswell, where the sea when it overtops the length of the beach can drain freely into Chiswell High Street then flow north into the Mere. It has been said that smugglers of old could quickly carry off their brandy and fishermen could bring their boats down them for safety, and in sunny weather wives would use them to carry their washing up onto the beach, where it would be laid out on the hot shingle to dry in the sun … The name of the wide ope beside the Chinese restaurant today defies identification, but may be called Lerret Ope. [The last] has been named No Ope by the present residents.'

Stow-on-the-Wold, Gloucestershire, with its ancient fairs, has alleys called the Tures, through which sheep were driven into the Market Square. Ilfracombe, Devon has its lanes; Bruton, Somerset its bartons; Lowestoft, Suffolk its scores. Liverpool has jiggers or jowlers; Hertfordshire has drokes; Great Yarmouth, Norfolk and Saffron Walden, Essex have rows. But in Chester, The Rows are medieval shopping arcades at first-floor level, reached by steps from the street.

Northumberland calls slender ways chares (cerr is Old English for narrow place or bend). In Newcastle, of the 21 chares that led out over the old piers as the waterfront pushed into the Tyne in the early 1800s, just a few survived the great fire of 1853 – notably The Chare, Manor, Prudhoe, Plummer and Broad Chares. Pudding Chare recalls not sweetmeats but Pow Dene, the small ravine and its stream now hidden below the pavement. With its deeply incised river, Newcastle also has many stepped alleys, such as Tuthill, Castle and Croft Stairs. In London the many stairs between buildings edging the Thames are remnants of working access to the river.

Whitby in Yorkshire developed on steep slopes dropping down to the river Esk, so steps and stairs are common – Salt Pan Well Steps, Cliff Steps and Chair Stairs (Jacob's Ladder to earlier generations). The town still has more than eighty named yards. They trace the narrow burgage plots or tofts (old freehold ownership patterns) at right angles to the street and give access to the dense infill of Georgian and Victorian houses. Arguments Yard (you can imagine: in the nineteenth century they were packed tight with families and had little sanitation) and many others are gone. Specific to Whitby are ghauts: explanations of the word are contested. The Oxford English Dictionary takes Hindi as the source, from *ghat* (mountain), morphing to a mountain pass and then a narrow way leading down to the river. Alan Whitworth offers a more domestic link: the word is locally pronounced as 'goat', an archaic name for stepping-stones, although lost are Tin Ghaut (T'Inn – the inn), Fish Ghaut and Collier's Ghaut, once leading to the water's edge. In Rochdale the name gauk may be related.

In Shrewsbury, where tourists enjoy exploring the convoluted and often stepped 'shuts' that ramify through the medieval town (Grope Lane, Coffee House Passage, St Julian's Steps, Castle Court), arguments rage about rights of way, gating and closure. The concern stemming from weekend wildness presumably was often revisited during the past thousand years, since one explanation of the name suggests that these lean lanes were closed at night.

ANCIENT TREES

Just as rocks keep a deep memory of the evolution of the earth, trees also compress history into their very being. That weight of knowledge is visible in old trees and it is part of England's special heritage to have more ancient trees than anywhere north of the Mediterranean except Greece.

We share with the Greeks, south Asians and many other cultures an appreciation and awe of ancient trees. They are full of enigma, capable in deciduous forms of apparent death and resurrection. They are the biggest beings we know; they stay rooted to the spot and in offering

permanence, longevity and grace they often organise the spirit of the place around them and are the reason why some places are where they are. They are the repository of memory.

These trees tell us of continuity and give us a glimpse of the old wild wood and ancient wood pasture. In cultural and ecological terms they are extraordinary. Oliver Rackham shook us by saying that *'ten thousand oaks of 100 years old are not a substitute for one 500-year-old oak'.*

Ancient trees are at the centre of their own ecological web. Some trees have lived so long that they harbour an extensive array of lichens and fungi as well as insects and micro-flora, some unique to themselves. Enormous and complex communities of symbiotic mycorrhizal root fungi are being discovered in the surrounding soil. The ancient oaks of the Wyre Forest in Shropshire and Worcestershire have become as Galapagan islands. In Herefordshire, those *'Old Men of Moccas Park'*, deferentially described by Francis Kilvert in his diary as *'those grey, gnarled, low-browed, knock-kneed, bowed, bent, huge, strange, long-armed, deformed, hunch-backed, misshapen oak men that stand waiting and watching century*

Dog Oak, Kentchurch, Herefordshire.

after century', have a far greater conservation status than as simple trees. The world population of the beetle *Hypebaeus flavipes* lives in just six Moccas Park oaks. The oaks and beeches of Windsor Great Park and Forest make that area the richest in northern Europe for invertebrates (two thousand species) and for fungi (one thousand species and counting). For bats and birds these trees offer habitation and food throughout the year.

Dendrologists can read a tree. Through the size and disposition of the rings laid down, one for each year, in its wood, they can tell something of the precipitation, the load of hungry insects and the level of happiness or distress of the growing organism. Real senility is easily apparent, but a measure of gnarledness translates with difficulty into specific age. Trees become more stable with time, they hollow naturally and become shorter but bulkier, and this natural engineering means that their annual rings cannot be counted.

Each tree is different. John White from the Forestry Commission has worked out a rule of thumb just for the Windsor oaks: a tree that is eighty inches in diameter at breast height with a girth of twenty feet and eight inches is around 433 years old; 120 inches in diameter with a girth of thirty feet eleven inches is 924 years old. Some of the oldest Windsor oaks are certainly more than a thousand years old.

Sitting inside the yew at Much Marcle, Herefordshire you feel the weight of centuries. It is thought to be fifteen hundred years old. Allen Meredith, whose yew work has sparked much investigation, thinks it may be five thousand years old; others have suggested nine thousand years.

The longevity stimulated by frequent cutting has meant that coppiced and pollarded trees number among our oldest. In Bradfield Woods, Suffolk an ash stool reaching 18 ½ feet across may be one thousand years old, and one small-leafed lime in Silk Wood, Westonbirt, Gloucestershire, 48 feet across, is thought to be six thousand years old.

These rich characters may have been nurtured by consistency of ownership – some areas of wood pasture have been in and out of the same family for a thousand years; most are in old deer parks or hunting forests, where stag-headed trees, humans and deer seem to merge:

There is an old tale goes, that Herne the Hunter,
Sometimes a keeper here in Windsor Forest,
Doth all the winter time, at still midnight,
Walk round about an oak, with great ragged horns…

WILLIAM SHAKESPEARE, from *The Merry Wives of Windsor*

In other places old trees have been retained to lend stature to a new park. Certain trees mark boundaries that date back to Saxon times. Some areas of land have never lost their status as commons, although few have enjoyed good woodmanship latterly, such as Epping Forest, Essex and Burnham Beeches, Buckinghamshire, where beech pollards may be four hundred years old.

Ted Green, an enthusiastic champion of ancient trees, who works as conservation consultant to Windsor Great Forest, is keen to understand the nine hundred mainly oak pollards that are more than five hundred years old. He wants to help them age and '*grow downwards*' – losing height, hollowing, putting on breadth and gravitas. They are being released from the pressing companionship of other trees. Haloes are cut around the ancients, since oak does not like to touch its neighbours, and more room to stretch is visibly reinvigorating even the oldest. Care is being taken not to expose the trees too much, because a sunburnt trunk begins to 'cook'. Preventing compaction above the roots helps them too, as fencing off the Major Oak in Sherwood Forest, Nottinghamshire from admirers has shown. Some trees are being selected to become successors to the ancients and their inhabitants and are being planted or left to grow nearby. Close observation and learning from countries where traditions remain unbroken is unlocking some of the secrets that were once every-day working wisdom in England.

Ironically, while wood folk who pollard and coppice have prolonged the lives of trees, foresters have been some of their worst enemies. The tunnel vision of those trained for timber growing during the twentieth century has defined 'over mature' trees as a waste of space. It is only in the past decade that the industry has begun to appreciate and champion their importance.

Any old tree is worth the space it occupies, whether a three-hundred-year-old sycamore or pear, a 150-year-old birch or a thousand-year-old yew. Giving names to these old characters endows them with some protection, but they should have the same conservation status as cathedrals and ancient monuments.

ARCADES

In 1990 a roof was completed over the length of Queen Victoria Street in Leeds. Brian Clarke's brilliantly coloured stained glass adds a new dimension to the resurgent reputation of the city and its unsurpassed shopping arcades. The area, now known as the Victoria Quarter, was first flamboyantly regenerated from a labyrinth of slaughter-houses and butchers' shops as the twentieth century began.

Inspired by Paris and, later, Italian cities, glassed-over arcades were seeping into English city life (the aristocratic Burlington Arcade in London opened in 1819 before Leeds built its first arcades towards the end of the nineteenth century. Four remain of the original eight.

Thornton's Arcade (1878) and Queen's Arcade (1889) were both designed by music hall architects and constructed where inn yards linked one street with another. The former was once Old Talbot Inn Yard, only fifteen feet wide, which joined Briggate with Lands Lane. The grand County Arcade, with its domes and mosaics, has been lavishly restored, having slipped into a decline that had left only six original shop fronts out of fifty. The Cross Arcade, birthplace of Marks and Spencer's Penny

Bazaar in 1904, was redeveloped in the 1990s to house the Harvey Nichols department store. The glass and steel entrance adds a fresh face to Briggate.

Elsewhere, compressing much into a little space to increase the commercial prospects of a city achieved elegance: in Lancashire, Accrington's Victorian Arcade (1896) is built over the river Hyndburn; Birmingham's Great Western Arcade (1875) is constructed over the railway; the Barton Arcade (1871) in Manchester is three storeys high.

There is another sort of arcade; the proportions are still grand but the feeling is of a noble cloister, since here buildings reach over the pavement and are supported by columns or arches that offer slats of shade and light. Inigo Jones's seventeenth-century Covent Garden in London was the earliest, based upon Palladio's Italian architecture. At the end of the twentieth century it has been joined by modern arcades at the back of the Royal Opera House, which finally complete the piazza. From Marlborough in Wiltshire to Saltburn in Yorkshire arcaded shops front the street and shelter shoppers from rain and sun.

BEACHCOMBING

It is hard to resist the pull of the beach as the tide recedes, always bringing something new from nature or from the flotsam and jetsam of humanity. In the West Country, the locals call it 'wrecking'. They are more likely to make the effort after a storm. Flotsam derives from the Anglo-Saxon word meaning 'to float', while jetsam defines things thrown from a boat, perhaps to lighten it in stormy conditions (from the French *jeter* – 'to throw'). In Cornwall they call them scummow.

Cornish people and those from the Isles of Scilly have a history of life-saving against the odds and avid retrieval of artefacts following storms and wrecks. The offshore rocks have long snagged nets and keels, barrels of brandy and rum; chests of wares from far-off places embellish many a story. Now it is more likely to be polystyrene, doomed to wander the seas forever, and bright yellow, red and blue plastics, together with driftwood, that liven up the strand line after a storm.

We can mourn organisms that have been ripped from their moorings or simply flung too high on the beach to return, but they fascinate natural historians. From Northumberland, Phil Gates described the carnage in his 'Country Diary' for *The Guardian*. '*Warkworth beach: the high tide and stormy seas had left tangled piles of kelp, torn from the seabed, all down the beach ... delicate hydroid colonies, sea squirts, sponges, whelks, hermit crabs and piles of sand mason worm cases.*' But, he added, '*the principal casualties were the starfish*', which cannot live out of water. Many of the prominent women naturalists of the early nineteenth century, such as Margaret Gatty, were seaweed collectors.

Along the coast near Lyme Regis, Dorset, geology buffs arrive in droves after word of big storms and rockfalls to seek out fossils emergent from their long sleep. The southern beaches of the Isle of Wight yield crunchies – smoothed vertebrae of dinosaurs; elephant bones are found on Norfolk's Overstrand; and on the edge of Northumberland, around Holy Island, St Cuthbert's beads – segments of crinoidal fossils – can be gleaned from the sand.

The glister of iron pyrites on the edge of rounded pebbles on the east Yorkshire coast may promise an embedded ammonite. From here to Essex, but particularly from Cromer in Norfolk to Felixstowe in Suffolk, you might get lucky after a big storm to find pieces of amber along the high-water mark, especially among the frondy seaweeds that are good at sweeping the sea floor. Amber is so light that it is flung high up the beach, perhaps having been loosened from submarine rock layers or having taken a long ride all the way from the Baltic.

The age and mixture of rocks around the south-west peninsula make for sparkling natural finds. Cornish diamonds (rock crystal – a sort of quartz) are quite widely scattered, while rare green and red serpentine is particular to Kynance Cove. From Penzance to Marazion, gems of agate, amethyst, citrine, carnelian and jasper are found. 'Plymouth limestone' and black glassy pieces are actually smelter's slag on the beaches around Penpol, possibly from ship's ballast. Along the Durham coast, once black with coal waste, it now requires concentration to turn up a fair piece of coal, while on the north side of Morecambe Bay, near Ulverston, Lancashire, the Town Beck chews on slag heaps that make for a milky tide.

In the past beachcombing supplemented income and kept families in fuel. In Dickensian London young children and women, called mudlarks, worked the Thames foreshore for anything they could sell, from lost coal to copper and old rope. Now anyone can walk the foreshore, but no one is allowed to dig without a Port of London Authority Permit. It is not easy to join the Society of Thames Mudlarks, who have permission to metal-detect and dig between the Tower and the Houses of Parliament.

Washed up whales and sturgeon, as Royal Fish, were claimed by the reigning monarch, although now the Natural History Museum has first refusal for whales. Objects that fall off ships must be declared to the Receiver of Wreck.

BEATING THE BOUNDS

The traditional day for beating the bounds of the parish was Holy Thursday, Ascension Day, forty days after Easter. It fell on the last of the Rogation Days – also called Cross Days, Gang Days or Grass Days in different places – the four days from the fifth Sunday after Easter (which itself falls on the Sunday after the first full moon following the vernal equinox).

Rogationtide, an ancient festival to invoke a blessing on fields, stock and folk, emerged after a sequence of natural disasters in fifth-century France. By the eighth century in England it involved parishioners 'ganging' (walking) after the Cross around the edge of the parish. This helped everyone to remember the boundaries before maps were commonplace.

Along the way prominent trees – Gospel Oaks – often became places for preaching.

The locations of various landmarks – stones, streams, hedges and ponds – were impressed upon children by ducking them in water, ritually beating them and then giving them a treat. In the twenty-first century anyone shopping on Ascension Day at Marks and Spencer in Oxford will see dignitaries and followers hitting a floor plaque with sticks, a formal reminder of the parish bounds of St Michael in the Northgate.

The Enclosures of the eighteenth and nineteenth centuries, which 'fixed' so many common lands into fields and bounds, killed many of the perambulations. But where they do survive they prove a sociable way of exploring. Afterwards you may be offered ganging beer and Rammalation biscuits, as they did at Aveton Gifford, Devon to celebrate the completion of their Parish Map in 1992.

In Rochester, Kent a boat is required every year to carry the Mayor of Medway, who holds the title of Admiral of the River, to trace the boundary down the centre of the estuary. His counterpart in the City of London does the same in the Thames. Every seventh year in Richmond, Yorkshire in September halberdiers and sergeants-at-mace lead an eighteen-mile perambulation and watch the water bailiff stride out into the river Swale.

In Cumberland and Northumberland it is still customary to Ride the Marches on horseback, as the parishes are large. At Berwick-upon-Tweed they have ridden the bounds on May Day annually since the reign of Henry VIII – in 2003 at least eighty riders followed Chief Marshal Alison Borthwick along a fifteen-mile stretch of Lamberton Moor.

Hodgson's *History of Northumberland* has the grand jury walking the boundaries of Morpeth and leaving a detailed description on 3 April 1758, including: '*and along by Watty's-hole, and so into the standers and through the garden in the same, walked over the water called Bowls-green Steps to the bounder stones*'. Today the Riding of the Bounds takes four hours, ending in the late afternoon with the St Mark's Day Races on Morpeth Common.

BELLS & BELL-RINGING

'Treble – going – gone' marks the start of something we take for granted, the sonorous sounds of churchbells. Yet nowhere else has developed such complex, tuneful ringing, save occasional churches in other English-speaking lands.

A ring of bells, together with the sound box of the tower, makes a complex musical instrument. In Europe the bell is still rung through ninety to 180 degrees. But the Reformation here led to a new, evolutionary path. Within the emergent Church of England successful experiments using wheels and levers meant that much more control could be exerted over the bell. Being rung round the whole circle enabled the bell to use its full voice and it could be started and stopped at bottom or top. This capacity to 'set the bell' led to the perfection of change ringing.

Joseph Strutt explained: *'Ringing of rounds; that is, sounding every bell in succession, from the least [the treble] to the greatest [the tenor], and repeating the operation, produces no variety … becomes tiresome: for which reason the ringing of changes has been introduced, wherein the succession of the bells is shifted continually, and by this means a varied combination of different sounds, exceedingly pleasant to the ear, is readily produced.'*

Many still agree. Across most of the country you will hear 'method' or 'scientific' ringing, which builds upon the mathematical explorations (by Richard Duckworth and Fabian Stedman) of *Tintinnalogia* in 1668 and *Campanalogia* in 1677. Their computations revealed that with twelve bells 479,001,600 unrepeated changes could be rung.

Since then hundreds of 'methods' have been elaborated, distinguished by names such as Stedman Doubles, Grandsire Triples and Bob Major.

St James' Church, Iddesleigh, Devon.

The number of bells is intimated in the title: Doubles means five bells; Minor, six; Triples, seven; Major, eight; Cators, nine; Royal, ten; Cinques, eleven; and Maximus, twelve. Changes such as London Surprise and Double Norwich Court Bob Major suggest where they were first perfected.

In the West Country the dialect varies. The styles of round ringing in Cornwall and call change ringing in Devon demand swift and crisp striking. The different way of raising the bells means that the con-catenation of sound starts immediately. Here, too, is the greatest concentration of churches with more than five bells: Somerset has 337, Devon 372. Compare this with 49 in Cumberland and Westmorland and sixteen in Northumberland (at the end of the twentieth century there were some 5,338 across England). While not all put in the same hours of practice as the Ancient Society of College Youths, a London society ringing since 1637, across the country societies of bell-ringers travel to ring bells for enjoyment and competition. On Dartmoor, Devon in 2004 and 2005 listening walks, recordings and celebrations of change ringing in all of the towers with five or more bells were initiated by Andy Stevens with Aune Head Arts.

Bells, rung to mark the time of day, times of prayer, events in the church calendar, rites of passage and festivities, from horse fairs to Pancake Day, have invisibly impressed themselves on many generations. The Curfew Bell sounded at eight or nine in the evening and is still rung in Chester, Stratford-upon-Avon in Warwickshire, Berwick-upon-Tweed in Northumberland and Chertsey in Surrey. The Morning Bell sum-moned labourers to work. This has proved contentious recently in Beaminster, Dorset, where through the summer the bell is still rung one hundred times just before 07.45, having shifted twice previously from 5am to 7am. One holidaymaker wrote in a visitors' book: '*please ring Quasimodo's neck!*'

The start of the year is traditionally marked by the ringing of bells. Margaret Baker in 1974 wrote of the Vale of Aylesbury in Buckinghamshire: '*Typifying the English tradition, one tower after another takes up the chain of sound, bell-music floating full and clear over the sleeping farms on the wind, tangling in branches of moonlit elms moving against the winter sky. Sometimes a muffled peal is first for the death of the old year, then as the last stroke of midnight dies away, the bells break into a merry open peal to welcome the new year.*'

Bells may be used for warning. Between 1940 and 1945 every bell tower was silenced, for use only in case of invasion. To ring out a celebration of the fiftieth anniversary of VE Day in 1995 carried that poignant reminder; at Wool in Dorset they took a minute longer to ring 5,040 Grandsire Doubles than their predecessors in 1945 – Philip Tocock conducted on both occasions. Many people of Lincolnshire carry terrifying memories of being woken by the frantic ringing of bells to alert them to the rising floods of 1953.

Few parts of the country lie outside a 'sound parish'. The 'bongs', as media folk call them, are broadcast by the BBC World Service across the globe, making Big Ben the most famous of bells – the more to surprise you when you hear them really ring out over the traffic in Westminster and on the Thames. Being born within the sound of London's Bow Bells (St Mary-le-Bow, Cheapside) traditionally marked the Cockney. On Highgate Hill, Dick and his cat were called back to the City on hearing Bow Bells call out: '*Turn again, Whittington, thrice Lord Mayor of London.*'

Bells have power, they hold people in their protection. Henry VIII knew well what he was about when he silenced Roman Catholic church bells; they remained without voice for three hundred years. Commentary on the stealing of church bells in nineteenth-century France suggests the seismic rocking of a community's sense of identity and belonging. Echoes of these kinds of fears persist in English legend. A bell, being stolen from Knowlton church in Dorset by the people of Sturminster Marshall, was dropped or hidden in the river Stour as they crossed White Mill Bridge. Salvaging it proved impossible, as it continuously slipped back into the river, where it supposedly remains. Elsewhere the devil is implicated in similar stories.

Memory or legend, both die hard. An earthquake is said to have devoured the whole village of Raleigh in Nottinghamshire and, until the nineteenth century, it was said that bells could be heard below the ground. Stories from Yarmouth in Norfolk and Tintagel in Cornwall tell of ringing being heard through the waves after boats carrying bells were lost at sea. The sound of bells haunts the sea off Selsey in Sussex, Whitby in Yorkshire and the Suffolk coast, where nine churches have slipped into the sea, together with the whole port of Dunwich, since medieval times.

BLUEBELLS

'*No woodland scene has the power to move the heart more than a bluebell wood in May,*' Peter Marren reminded us. In spring, the floor of a bluebell wood becomes a carpet, a lake, a sea of azure, as the massed blooms merge and shimmer like a pool of water.

Only ramsons (wild garlic) have the same capacity as bluebells to take possession of whole woods. But bluebells outdo them, providing one of the most glorious spectacles in the botanical world. '*No other country has them on so large a scale,*' said ecologist Oliver Rackham. Spring is their season because bluebells are shade evaders, seizing the chance to grow and flower before the trees sprout leaves and when more than a third of the sun's rays can still reach the woodland floor. Numbers multiply where recent thinning or coppicing has let in more light.

Rejecting the extremes of both dry and waterlogged soils, bluebells flourish among all manner of trees, on moderately acid, sandy loams as

Haddon Hill Wood, East Knoyle, Wiltshire.

well as in clay woods and chalky hangers. Among the best, photographer Bob Gibbons reckons, are West Woods in Wiltshire, Hayley Wood in Cambridgeshire, Tortoiseshell Wood in Lincolnshire and the woodlands along the Ribble valley east of Preston in Lancashire. Bluebells even thrive on Atlantic coastal cliffs, beside the ruins of Tintagel Castle in Cornwall, for instance. The hedge banks and deep-set lanes of Devon delight with the good companions of bluebell, red campion and stitchwort.

On the eastern side of England especially they have long been taken as a sign of old, undisturbed woods, with bluebells in hedgerows or bracken testifying to woods that have disappeared. Persistent plants, they shade out wildflower competitors through sheer force of numbers, and stockpile poisonous glycosides that deter foraging animals. As a result, some bluebell carpets, as Marren observed, '*may be unfathomably old, waxing and waning according to the vicissitudes of light, climate and woodmanship, but essentially changing little*'.

Bumblebees appreciate their nectar, advertised by the blooms' spicy, balsamic perfume. The Elizabethan herbalist Gerard knew it as the English Jacinth, or Blue Harebell, and reckoned the flowers had '*a strong sweet smell, somewhat stuffing the head*'. The pear-shaped bulbs once generated starch to stiffen Elizabethan ruffs, while the flower stalks exuded a versatile glue used for binding books or fixing feathers on arrows.

Wildflowers with a rich folklore, names include Granfer Griggles and Goosey Ganders, shared with the early purple orchid. West Country bluebells have long been away with the fairies: local names include fairy cap in Wiltshire, fairy bells and fairy thimbles in Somerset and fairy cup, fairy ringers and ding-dongs in Dorset.

CAIRNS

At the summit of large hills and mountains, a pile of stones commemorates the achievement of reaching the top or acts as a waymark, informal trig point, memorial, boundary mark or beacon. Many are just small mounds of stones, a gathering of whatever is to hand, but some are landmarks in their own right.

On the Yorkshire/Westmorland border, on a hill overlooking the Vale of Eden, a line of stone cairns on the skyline *'stand like sentries on a rampart at the northern edge of the Yorkshire Dales'*. The Nine Standards Rigg inspired artist Andy Goldsworthy, who lived in Brough in his early twenties: *'I could look across at Hartley Fell, and see the Nine Standards … They have all been added to and taken away from by visitors over the years, and this change adds to their life; they have "grown" there over a long time, where the stone is plentiful and suitable. What is really interesting was the way that they affected the valley, the way they dominated the valley … The ones on the top act for me like sentinels, they look like a group of people and there is a protective side to them.'* They proved seminal, Andy says: *'I have made cones all over the world and they are like markers to my travels.'*

Describing his walks in the Lake District, Alfred Wainwright commented on the many cairns at the summits. At the top of Hopegill Head he noticed thirty to forty swifts wheeling round the cairn and then round his head as he drew nearer: *'This was the only time I came within five yards of a summit cairn yet was unable to reach it: that short distance was made untenable by the diving swifts, but I was near enough to see the pile of stones was covered by flying ants and that I was disturbing a feast. On other occasions I have found colonies of winged ants on summit cairns but unattended by predators, and once on the top of Caw in the Duddon Valley I found the cairn completely plastered with ladybirds, the stones appearing to be stained a bright red. These migrating*

Nine Standards Rigg, near Kirkby Stephen, Westmorland.

flights of insects seem to have a liking for coming to rest at summit cairns, bless their little hearts, just as I have.' Like us, migratory birds and insects use cairns as navigational aids.

Blawearie cairns on Bewick Moor in Northumberland have a different history: a jet and shale necklace, a flint knife and a food vessel were found within them. Archaeologists know cairns as round mounds of stone dating from the Bronze Age and accommodating a single burial, though there may be one or more secondary burials placed in the mound at later dates. Barbara Bender adds that *'these burials were complete and were often accompanied by fine beakers, archery equipment and gold ornaments. Clearly the most important people were placed below the mounds.'* In the South West, ring cairns are widely found on the moors; a fine example exists at Cheriton Ridge on Exmoor.

Gough's Memorial of 1890 on the top of Helvellyn is one of many cairns built in memory of the dead. An engraved stone slab backed by rough stones, it recounts how Gough's dog stayed faithfully beside his master three months after he had died close to the summit. Whatever their origin, however old or new, we can agree with Wainwright that *'To pull down a summit cairn is a sacrilege'.*

CANALS

Where there are no rivers, they have been created, ever since the Romans linked the Trent and Witham rivers in Lincolnshire by the Fossdyke. The 'cut', or canal, came to prominence in the mid-eighteenth century, built for moving inland coal to industrial centres and ports. Merseyside and Manchester benefited, and other trades followed: pottery on the Trent and Mersey; copper at Tavistock in Devon. Canals came to Shrewsbury, Coventry and Birmingham, which had 159 miles of them by 1898 – many are still in use. The military built a canal from Sussex to Kent, for troop movements, supplies and to create an obstacle for invaders.

A new linear particularity was laid across the country, in new byways (towpaths), bridges and buildings constructed from newly accessible materials. Round houses were built for employees on the Thames and Severn; barrel-roofed cottages and delicate split bridges lined the Stratford-upon-Avon in Warwickshire; ornate classical lodges appeared on the Gloucester and Sharpness. The Kennet and Avon wharf at Devizes, Wiltshire brought fashionable Bath stone for the town's new buildings. The Grand Union, linking London with the Midlands, was the most extensive network in the country, its unique features including Lombardy poplars and pollarded willows along its towpaths, as well as mooring bollards, pumping stations and mileposts. Where buildings were required and the right clay could be found, local brick works appeared. At Foxton, Leicestershire a brick works was the starting point for a small community that developed to service canal travellers.

Canal people decorated everything – their narrow boats, with bold lettering and floral decorations, and their domestic ware, with brightly coloured paintings, mainly of roses and castles on dark backgrounds. At Cut End, Measham in Derbyshire glazed brown Measham Teapots (known as 'barge teapots'), with moulded and glazed decorations and a miniature teapot on the lid as a handle, were made until 1939.

The canal network decayed once the railways took their trade. Some were completely overbuilt, others changed their nature. Part of the Wiltshire and Berkshire canal is now Swindon's shopping precinct The Parade. Their revival for leisure purposes during the twentieth century sprang from enthusiasts' zeal. Linton Lock in Yorkshire was among the earliest restoration projects in 1949. By 1962 there were two thousand miles of network, which British Waterways was created to manage.

Many remain sleepy and tranquil; wildlife has returned both to disused and restored stretches of cut. Water voles have reappeared; there have

Canal ware.

been otters on the Pocklington canal in Yorkshire. Some are the focus of festivals, boat galas and town fairs, such as Skipton and Standedge in Yorkshire, Foxton Locks in Leicestershire and Gas Street Basin in Birmingham. In 2001 the Association of Inland Navigation Authorities proposed a number of projects to revive and make links between canals. These would bring a new cohesion to the network, but also cause ecological concern if they were to move and mix water on a serious scale between catchments.

CHURCHES

We take our parish churches for granted, yet they mark out the country and the city in remarkable ways. Built to command respect and awe and draw the eye to the heavens, they are impressive even now, to the extent that they form literal landmarks for mariners and migrating birds. The tiered contours of St Bride's spire in Fleet Street provokes any London taxi driver worth 'The Knowledge' to comment on how it inspired the shape of the wedding cake. Breedon church is vulnerable above the quarry face in Leicestershire; Great Salkeld in Cumberland is simple and sturdy. St Mary the Virgin in Shrewsbury is lit with windows of five centuries of stained glass, and we agree with Simon Jenkins that Christchurch Priory in Hampshire is, simply, sensational.

Christianity had spread through urban Roman Britain, but it took another wave of influence from the reconstructed continental church, from the late sixth century, to establish Christianity across England. Pre-Christian practices and Celtic sensibilities nevertheless continued to play an important role. Churches are orientated towards the east. Those

Zennor, Cornwall.

dedicated to St Michael are invariably on significant hills that can catch the rising of the sun, a legacy of Egypt, Osiris and the Coptic church – think of St Michael's Mount in Cornwall and the skyline around Glastonbury in Somerset. Churches devoted to St Mary, the mother of Christ, are often situated beside springs.

Many believe that the positioning of churches owed much to an intention to take over the power of the pre-Christian sites, to insinuate and absorb. The yew trees at Darley Dale in Derbyshire and at Clun in Shropshire may pre-date their stone companions by two thousand years. Ruined Knowlton in Dorset sits quietly in the centre of a circular neolithic earthwork, and the church at Rudston, Yorkshire, keeps company with a prehistoric monolith nearly twenty feet in height.

Although some churches were built to stand alone – such as those of the Charnwood Forest in Leicestershire – following the enclosure of 1830, there are many isolated churches that tell of the contraction, desertion and mobility of settlements over the centuries.

Early worship was outside beside a stone cross or in small wooden buildings. The minsters were the mother churches, centres of evangelism; their names linger in the towns – Wimborne Minster in Dorset, Kidderminster in Worcestershire. Later came the churches built by Saxon lords – Escomb in County Durham is a rare survivor. By 1066 most people could walk to a church and some were within the sound of church bells and sight of a tower. The close pattern of parishes and church sites was laid.

Rebuilding took place at many churches with the coming of the Normans and again as the wool, worsted (in the East) and broadcloth (in the South West) trades of the fourteenth and fifteenth centuries, and

Elton, Gloucestershire.

later economic booms, offered money and energy for refashioning. Then, in 1539, England broke with the Church of Rome and English churches fragmented into yet further idioms. Victorian generosity founded new chapels and churches, but the overzealous 'restoration' of Tewkesbury Abbey in Gloucestershire prompted William Morris to create the Society for the Protection of Ancient Buildings, because all the accretions of intervening ages were being wiped away in a misguided attempt to recapture someone's idea of the purity of the original.

Once the centralised cultural grip of the Middle Ages began to diminish, the building of a church was an expression as much of wealth and building skills as it was of the glory of God. With the interest in bells came the need for height and the unparalleled flowering of one of England's greatest wonders – the parish church with tower or spire.

Towers predominate, although spires, with myriad variations, have a heartland in the east Midlands. Yorkshire, with a tradition of towers, has one of the most elegant spires, in Patrington. Simple gabled towers, mostly of the thirteenth and fourteenth centuries, looking like tall, medieval square silos with pitched roofs, are found along a line linking Somerset and south Lincolnshire. They coincide with the Lias limestone, poorer for agriculture and wealth generation and hence associated with plainer building techniques – the simplicity of Fingest church is a real prize in its now opulent Buckinghamshire village.

So near and yet so different, polygonal towers, influenced by continental Europe and dating from the twelfth to sixteenth centuries, march along the line of fine building stone from Norfolk, through Ely and Peterborough, to Somerset. Christopher Wren picked up the style in some of his London churches a century later.

The timber towers of Worcestershire, often separate from the nave, as at Pirton and Warndon, delight with simplicity and pattern. The annual rings in the timbers of the freestanding bell tower at Yarpole, Herefordshire tell us that the oaks were cut in 1195, setting a local style seen again in Pembridge, Bosbury and Richard's Castle. At Greenstedjuxta-Ongar in Essex stands the oldest of wooden churches. Its nave is lined with split oak and it has a white, weather-boarded tower.

Somerset's large, elegant towers have elaborate pinnacles at each top corner and fine parapets. There is variety across the county, from Mells in the Mendips to Bishops Lydeard (with a red sandstone tower) in the Quantocks, and variation within and between. Here the silhouettes of the Perpendicular towers are ornamented by carvings of mythical birds and beasts, locally called hunky punks. Some leaning steeples persist, as at St Peter's in Barnstaple, Devon, Temple Church in Bristol and the famed twisted spire at Chesterfield in Derbyshire.

Lichenologists love stone churches; more than a third of all lichens present in Britain have been recorded on church and in graveyard. Their great age has allowed these very slow-growing plants to spread undisturbed for centuries. Leaky pipes and gutters, while foreshortening the church's life, increase the range of species – typically thirty to forty species may be found. The mix and age of the stone and the church's east–west orientation offer a variety of habitats, particularly in the contrast offered by north- and south-facing roofs and walls. Some lichens are so precise in their needs that they tell of the invisible variation in stone. In Northamptonshire, *Hypocenomyce scalaris* will grow only on the local sandy ironstone, and Sulgrave church demonstrates colourful patina, with yellow lichens at the top of the tower, white lichens on the string course, many-coloured communities on south-facing walls and grey-green communities on the north side.

The simple broached and crooked stone spire of St Enodoc leans into the dunes by the beach at Daymer Bay, Cornwall. In the eighteenth and nineteenth centuries sand overwhelmed the church, to the extent that the locals called it the 'sinkininny church' and the vicar was lowered in through the roof once a year to maintain its consecration. Lovingly cleared and renovated by careful Victorians, it is enfolded now by sand-holding tamarisk, that candy-floss-pink flowering tree that softly coats our warmer coasts. It is fitting that John Betjeman, who so idiosyncratically celebrated the richness of our building heritage, lies here, bringing others to a favourite corner of England.

Around two thousand churches and chapels have been made redundant during recent years; some now house apartments, art centres, places of work or leisure. The church may or may not still be at the religious centre of its parish, but it often forms the aesthetic focus and performs a spiritual role. It behoves all who care for the embodied history in each one to think creatively about the future of these exquisite buildings in a secular society.

CLOUDS

'*Mackerel sky and mare's tails, make lofty ships carry low sails.*' Seafarers know their clouds, and so do farmers. '*When clouds appear like rocks and towers, the earth's refreshed by frequent showers.*' Descriptive names and chronic observation are part of the weather lore that drives English bus-stop conversation and universal weather forecasting.

Strange to say, a full lexicon of cloud names does not seem to have come down to us – lamb's wool sky, mackerel sky, mare's tails, overcast, rain cloud, stacken cloud, thunder cloud and wane cloud are about the extent of it. That is, until 1802, when Luke Howard named the clouds. He had closely observed their shapes and altitude for years, and, filled with the light of Linnaeus, classified their patterns and gave them Latin names. The success of this venture permeates meteorology: what Howard did was to help us see the invisible – to begin to understand the atmosphere.

In 2002 he was remembered; his old house in Tottenham, north London now carries a blue plaque. At the time his fame went wide. Goethe lauded him in four poems: '*As clouds ascend, are folded, scatter, fall,/ Let the world think of thee who taught it all.*' Shelley, too, was moved to precision in 'The Cloud', and he offers in almost riddle form a fine evocation of the water cycle:

I am the daughter of earth and water,
And the nursling of the sky;
I pass through the pores of the ocean and shores;
I change, but I cannot die.

John Constable's sketchbooks of 1821/2 are filled with exquisite observations of clouds over London. From the fields off Prospect Walk on Hampstead Heath he painted more than a hundred studies of *'noble clouds and effects of light'*, the notes and dates giving us a diary of two summers, his close observation built upon a childhood of intimacy with the wide and often wild Suffolk skies. His paintings of Weymouth Bay from the Dorset coast demonstrate something we have all done, which is to watch the weather going or coming.

Sometimes clouds redefine the landscape. Edward Burra's painting *Near Whitby, Yorkshire, 1972* has a road, edged by plunging moorland slopes, running into numinous mist-cum-cloud. Memorable are the days when hills become islands and new shorelines seem to edge the valley of the Trent seen from Charnwood, Leicestershire, when cloud sinks into the bottoms and leaves the high places to gloat in the sun.

There are repeated local rhymes that warn of weather to come. *'If Simonside has her nightcap on in the morning, it's sure to rain'* is one saying from Cambo in Northumberland, while in Devon they say, *'When Hall Down wears a hat / Let Kenton beware of a skat'* (shower).

One can become mesmerised by clouds: by high, wispy cirrus made more from ice crystals than water vapour; lower duvets of stratus; heaped cumulus – flat-bottomed, discrete and fluffy, suggesting settled weather – or cumulonimbus, big and billowing, threatening rain. Seen from a plane they make their own fabulous landscapes and, from the ground, what you will:

HAMLET. *Do you see yonder cloud that's almost in shape of a camel?*
POLONIUS. *By th' mass, and 'tis like a camel, indeed.*

HAM. *Methinks it is like a weasel.*
POL. *It is backed like a weasel.*
HAM. *Or like a whale?*
POL. *Very like a whale ...*

WILLIAM SHAKESPEARE, from *Hamlet*

COMMONS

Raggle-taggle open land with a wild, unkempt look may spring to mind, but the variety of common land ranges from thousands of mountain-top acres in the Lake District to slivers of roadside in Herefordshire. Each contributes to the feel of the place. The 'Strays' of York are now used for town recreation rather than grazing. Northamptonshire has virtually no common land, whereas great expanses of unenclosed common cover the uplands of the northern counties, as well as Bodmin Moor in Cornwall and Dartmoor in Devon.

The name describes not the land but the rights over it. Common rights are of great antiquity, perhaps pre-dating private property, remnants from a time before the Normans made land-grabbing the sport of kings, courtiers and church. From town fairground to unfenced heath, 'the common' is shorthand for something made complicated by time, change and struggle. For centuries commons have been areas of land over which the specific rights of local people have persisted over someone else's 'soil'. These rights made the difference between starvation and survival.

Commons are still owned by a lord of the manor, who now may be a local authority, and it is only since the Countryside and Rights of Way Act 2000 came into force that the right to walk on registered common land has been open to all. The Open Spaces Society has been campaigning for this for more than a century.

Apart from new-won access to air and exercise, the range of rights is manifold. The most widespread are to estovers (pollarded branches, underwood for fencing, bracken and gorse for bedding); housebote (bigger timbers for repair or building); pannage (running pigs under woodland to take fallen acorns and beechmast); pasture (stock grazing); piscary (fishing); turbary (peat digging for fuel); and the right of common in the soil (sand, gravel and stone). They are matched by rigorous rules, such as the stinting or regulation of stock numbers or grazing hours, set by the commoners or by court leet. The landholder usually retains rights of minerals and shooting and may or may not share some of the common rights.

In 1963 Dudley Stamp computed that of England's 1,055,000 acres of common land, two-thirds lay in the upland moors and fells of Durham, Cumberland, Lancashire, Northumberland, Yorkshire and Westmorland, and that of the lowland commons nearly half lay within fifty miles of London. It was around that time that commons registration began. Now we seem only to have 370,000 hectares (914,307 acres). Yes, we changed measurement systems in between, but this is not a European conspiracy. Many commons were simply not registered: to Dorset's shame, for example, a large number simply faded away.

The Surrey heaths have a long history of recreational use, with more common land owned by local authorities than any other county. This reflects pioneering work done by the Commons Preservation Society and the National Trust. Chobham Heath, busy with human toil since the Stone Age, is now criss-crossed by pipelines, aerial lines, railway lines and the M3 motorway, as well as footpaths and bridleways. Here the Bagshot Sands, rendered even less fertile by the removal of trees as early as Neolithic times, are typical of manorial 'waste' – land marginal to cultivation.

In Dorset's Blackmore Vale, wayside common land borders roads now metalled but once so soggy that wide swathes were left for carts to find their own way through. Cut for hay, left for nature or occasional use by travellers and Romani, some were squatted long ago and have thin cottages with stretched gardens along the roadside.

The lack of commons in the midland counties dates from the century following 1750 and reflects the greater success here of landowners enclosing the land for agriculture. Today, farming is changing again, and its fluctuating patterns are echoed in the look and ecology of the land. Many lowland heath commons suffer from under-grazing, while upland commons may be over-grazed; both threaten vulnerable fauna and flora.

'Commons left free in the rude rags of nature', as John Clare had them, may have been on the poorest land, and this is what makes them ecologically rich. Mellis Green, a mile long and 174 acres, is the biggest grazing common in Suffolk. It is a nature reserve: 158 recorded species of flowering plants, many butterflies, owls, skylarks, kingfishers, water voles and pigmy shrews are all desirable neighbours. But the Suffolk Wildlife Trust, to whom the lord of the manorship was given in 1989, spent the early part of the new millennium hassling house owners around the green for amounts of money for vehicular access rights across the common to their houses, some of which are hundreds of years old. Roger Deakin, a resident, says in doing this 'the Suffolk Wildlife Trust may have surrendered the moral authority it needs to safeguard the vulnerable historic landscape'; the people who edge the common ought to be its chief allies.

Survival of commons requires people to work together to practise appropriate farming, wildlife and recreational activities. English Nature is busy learning how in the Yorkshire Dales, where scars, screes and limestone pavement offer varied calcareous habitats, with plants such as bloody cranesbill and bird's-eye primrose among the grassland, mire and juniper shrub, enjoyed by the northern brown argus butterfly and birds such as curlew and wheatear. Agreements with grazier commoners have already seen the re-emergence of juniper on Moughton Common.

Every common has its own story to tell, of great struggles in different centuries between lords of the manor and commoners. The Town Moor in Newcastle, where travellers and showmen arrive in late June for the great fair, the Hoppings, is owned by the city council. The commoners carry the title Freemen of the City and have grazing rights over some of the 350 acres. As the city grew this expanse was maintained as open land because the commoners fought for their rights. The struggles never end. Town Moor has been made to accommodate formal recreation and sports grounds, parks and allotments, although the Friends of Town Moor have successfully countered the relocation of the Newcastle United Football Club from St James' Park.

Lord Thomas Maryon Wilson tried for half a century from 1818 to enclose Hampstead Heath. He took such quantities of sand as to change the shape of the land and tried repeatedly to introduce Acts of Parliament to build. The commoners were, however, men of means and connections, resisting at every turn. After his death the land was bought by the Metropolitan Board of Works, to which it added Parliament Hill in 1889. By 1924, with the addition of Kenwood, the Heath reached eight hundred acres. It is just one of the jewels in the capital city's crown of commons, many safeguarded by the Metropolitan Commons Act of 1866, which prevented enclosure of land within a fifteen-mile radius of Charing Cross. It is now managed by the Corporation of London, as is the greatest of the Essex commons, Epping Forest – five thousand acres of ancient pollarded hornbeams and oaks preserved by the Epping Forest Act *'for the enjoyment, in perpetuity, by the citizens of London'*.

Having been a place for army training in the First World War, then bought by the old Borough of Newbury in 1939 for recreation, Greenham and Crookham Commons in Berkshire were requisitioned for the war effort. In 1941 an airfield was built and after the war the Air Ministry let it to the US Air Force. In the early 1980s this became the focus of a protest against cruise missiles and nuclear war. Women from across the country created a peace camp, lived here, penetrated the base, danced on missile silos and created a vortex of (dis)enchantment.

> *Who stole the Goose off the Common?*
> *Who stole the Common off the Goose?*
> *Who stole the land for airfields?*
> *Who turned the scientists loose?*

DENNIS GOULD, from 'Greenham Common Blues'

Feminists, anarchists, pacifists, ecologists, Buddhists and Quakers joined a long roll call of civil disobedience to prevent a final extinguishing of rights and to win back the common for the people. By 8 April 2000, the perimeter fence had been completely removed – seventeen years after hundreds of women had been arrested for cutting down five of its nine miles. The Greenham and Crookham Commons Act was passed in 2002, guiding restoration, conservation and rights for public access to this place of ecological, cultural and historical significance.

The concrete from the runway, the longest in Europe, has been crushed and used to build a local school. Some has remained and been grassed over – the contrast with the indigenous acid soils produces an unexpected mix of flora. The brooding missile silos, clustered and grassed over like giant barrows, still crouch behind wire, and barn owls have moved in. Walking here with the smell of gorse, the sounds of larks, the sight of a hare, the laughter of children and the pounding of jogging feet, anyone now can be part of the process of reclaiming this place, despite its ghosts, for nature and people.

CORNISH PASTIES

The Cornish pasty is a meal in itself. It was invented to fit into a pocket and be eaten without a knife or fork. These are the qualities that made it the staple diet of Cornish tin- and copper-mine workers, blacksmiths and engineers in the first half of the nineteenth century.

The traditional Cornish pasty is made with thick, shortcrust pastry

and filled with raw chopped onions, potatoes, swedes (known in Cornwall as turnips), skirt or chuck steak and seasoning. The pastry is rolled to about a quarter of an inch thick and cut into round, plate-sized portions; the filling is put onto one half and the rest of the pastry folded over, the edges dampened and crimped with fingers and thumb. Some prefer to place the filling in the centre of the pastry and have the 'seam' at the top. Initials might be carved into one corner. It is glazed with egg or milk, a slit is made on the top to let out steam, and it is baked in a hot oven for about twenty minutes and then at a lower temperature for a further forty.

There used to be many variations on the fillings – beef and potatoes, fish, pork, cheese and onion, egg and bacon, rabbit, whatever was to hand. Some combined savoury and sweet ingredients, the pudding half of apple, jam or treacle separated by an internal portion of pastry, to be washed down with sweet tea – this is reminiscent of the Bedfordshire clanger.

The pasty became known as 'Cornish' in Victorian times by visitors to the county. Now three million pasties are made in Cornwall every week, although ninety per cent are sold outside the county. Their makers obtained European Protected Geographical Indication status in 2011, so that only pasties made in Cornwall can be called by that name.

COTTAGES

The dark, smoky, damp and overcrowded cottage, originally the home of the poor peasant, labourer or miner and his extended family, offered simple shelter and sometimes a place to work. Building materials came from nearby, some to be used time and again. William Wordsworth opened our eyes to these buildings: *'these humble dwellings remind the contemplative spectator of a production of Nature, and may (using a strong expression) rather be said to have grown than to have been erected; – to have risen, by an instinct of their own, out of the native rock – so little is there in them of formality, such is their wildness and beauty'.*

The cottage is much loved for its honesty, simplicity and truth to locality. Its drawbacks have had money and technical sophistication poured upon them, making it comfortable now to let the cottage evoke a time of 'harmony with the land' for which we long to return (never having to suffer its realities). It is telling that the two most popular house names are The Cottage and Rose Cottage. Other attractions lie in its adaptability. Its stories are felt, age is seen to have gathered, and longevity, back beyond even an eighteenth-century exterior, may be hidden behind additions and adaptations.

Cottages, farmhouses and farm buildings, more than any other building types, bring stone and earth to life and demonstrate all kinds of local nuances learned from experience of the place by craftsmen and builders. In turn, the flavour of the locality is heightened. The legacy of variation demonstrates the richness of geological sequences and rising economic fortunes to be read in periods of rapid building and the extending use of local stone, brick or earth. That is, until the 1850s, when mass production and the railways brought cheaper and more uniform bricks and Welsh slate to all but the most inaccessible parts.

Cottages had sprung up along spring lines, around village greens, by mineral workings and woodland edges. If you could put up a building on common land in one night, with a bit of thatch on it in Devon, or just a smoking chimney by dawn in Herefordshire and Shropshire, then you earned squatters' rights to stay.

Where large pieces of timber were available, early one-room cottages were made either with cruck frames, resembling a big A, with walls of wattle and daub in the West Midlands and the North, or with a box frame, more frequently found in southern and eastern England. Cottages with thick, unbaked earth walls or cob, protected by plaster

Kingston, Devon.

Liverton Mines, Yorkshire.

North Pennines.

Skirmett, Buckinghamshire.

Cowden, Kent.

and limewash and a thatched roof of reeds, straw, gorse, bracken, heather, brushwood or turf, with overhanging eaves, were common in the South West, East Anglia and parts of the Midlands.

By the end of the 1600s, cottages were being built of locally quarried uncut (rubble) stone if it was available. Bricks appeared in cottages in the 1700s, usually handmade locally – the range of size, shape and colour has contributed to subtle differences in and between places. Brick noggin (an infilling of bricks often placed in a herringbone pattern), if it could be afforded, began to replace wattle and daub or cob. At the same time, clay tiles and pantiles began to oust thatch in some areas.

The shape and mass of cottages vary. Some are hard-edged and precise, such as the long rows of single-storey stone and slate cottages in Northumberland, built by landowners to house their workers. In the Derbyshire and Yorkshire sand and gritstone areas, the workability of the stone makes for solid lintels, window and door surrounds and the little shoulders or 'kneelers' protruding from the gable parapet. Cottages sharing walls were common, as they were cheaper to build and kept each other warm or cool.

Others appear sculpted and are situated less rigidly, face or gable to the road, their plasticity deriving from softer materials of cob or thatch. Peter Mason wrote: '*The most commonly occurring small house type in Hampshire is the thatched, one-and-a-half-storeyed building, often called a "bun-cottage"*.' John and Jane Penoyre observed: '*With eyebrows of thatch over the half-dormers and their soft, brown, rounded outlines curving down over their half-hipped ends, the cottages seem more roof than wall, an effect heightened by the technique, logical in a moulded material, of extending the thatch downwards to cover the porch.*'

Homeworking was once commonplace – jewellery in Birmingham, saddlery in Walsall and silk in Leek, Staffordshire. 'Cottage industry' could make demands on the shapes of buildings. Weavers' windows betray the need for extra light in upstairs rooms, as in Saddleworth and Thurlstone in Yorkshire and Macclesfield in Cheshire. Plate glass for windows became available for labourers' cottages in the 1800s, replacing small panes of bottle glass in lead casings.

Cottages built for lock keepers and level-crossing lookouts are visibly tied to their time, task and place, even though other evidence may be long gone. Enlightened philanthropists built estate and model villages in the eighteenth and nineteenth centuries, some with exaggerated rustic charm, known as cottage orné. The Victorian picturesque and Gothic Revival brought romantic cottages with tall chimneys, intricate tiling, thatched roofs with low eaves, dormer windows and carved barge-boards – more for the squire to savour than for the incumbent.

During the past decade a new generation of cottages has begun to appear. At Osmington and Corfe in west Dorset, South Creake in Norfolk and Bishop's Mead in Chelmsford, Essex, builders are leaning on the vernacular, but with the market in mind. A new generation of people, some working from home, is buying two-storey buildings, sometimes helping to keep small quarries open and local craftsmanship alive, while embracing new, energy-conscious technologies.

COUNTIES

In 1974 Avon, Cleveland, Cumbria, Merseyside, Humberside, South Yorkshire and the West Midlands stared back at us from administrative maps. Greater London had appeared in 1965. Rutland, Huntingdonshire, Westmorland, East Yorkshire and Middlesex – *'that most hardly used of all counties'*, as Betjeman put it – seemed to evaporate, and other parts of the familiar jigsaw changed shape. But many of us had not moved an inch and the unsettling truth became clear two decades later, when things changed again – these were just passing clouds. Our 'real' counties, 39 shapes, historic bounds of cultural life and identity, had never gone away.

The Association of British Counties has persuaded us of the usefulness of discerning between counties (historic counties), administrative counties and ceremonial counties (the domain of the Lord Lieutenant, which in Derbyshire, for example, includes the City of Derby). All are constructs, but the historic counties tell us about deep identity, having earned credibility through continued use over a thousand years or more. Kent is the oldest entity to be recorded, first in 55 BC, the land of the Cantii tribe, whose name could come from Celtic *canto*, an edge or rim (geographically appropriate), or from *caint* – 'open country'.

As Oxford and Cambridge blues compete along the Thames, reference to the Middlesex side and the Surrey side reminds us of the historic configuration, the boundary between the people of the Middle Saxons and the people of Suthrige – the region south of the Thames. Rivers and hills are often taken as borders and boundaries. But there are traces of old political rivalries, too, some of which may reach back to Celtic times.

The historic counties.

As Norman Davies writes: '*The transformation of the chaotic patchwork of statelets into a map containing fewer but much larger and more integrated political cultural units was the work of half a millennium. It was not a fore-gone conclusion. Through a thousand military conflicts, marriages, mergers and mishaps, the teeming territories of the fifth century amalgamated in the course of two hundred years to form a dozen rival kingdoms. After two hundred years more, the kingdoms of the seventh century had been still further reduced, leaving two distinct zones – one predominantly Celtic, the other exclusively Germanic.*'

In the Germanic zone, smaller units – Saxon *scirs* (shires) and Norse *jarldoms* (earldoms) under the Danelaw – appear in written documents: for example, East Seaxe (Essex) in 604; Beaurrucsir (Berkshire), referring to a wooded hill, in 860; Scrobbesbyrigscir (Shropshire) – the shire of Shrewsbury, Latin Civitas Scrobbensis, 'the city around the scrub folk' – in 1006.

The counties of England emerged out of the Norman administrative system, based in most of the country on these shires or provinces, arranged around kings, upon peoples and obligations of providing soldiers and taxes. The lands of the middle, south and east Saxons were governed as the shires of Middlesex, Sussex and Essex; the 'folk of the north and south' were resolved into the shires of Norfolk and Suffolk. Wessex under Alfred had long been divided into smaller *scirs*. The Celts were confined by the Saxons to the 'land of the foreigners' – Kerno, kern-wealh or Cornwall. Northumbria and Yorkshire were already defined and the Mercian midlands had been divided in the tenth century. As he drew the country together, all William the Conqueror had left to delineate were Durham, Cumberland, Westmorland, Lancashire and Rutland, with his counts at their helm.

And so the county remained for centuries, persisting for the most part through the Victorian invention of a new administrative system with elected members, but with cities now jostling for power. Closer to our time, years of debate over what to put where was resolved by a change of government in 1970. The Conservatives recoiled from radical rewriting of administrative boundaries and settled for a partial and inconsistent rejigging. In 1974, when new two-tier structures and unitary authorities appeared, people felt their counties had been dismembered.

Lancastrians were upset by the inclusion of Lancashire, North of the Sands, in Cumbria. Confusion persists. In criticising Common Ground's original england-in-particular.info website, gazetteer Michael Dutson was more restrained than some: '*Lancastrians are proud of their county and its achievements and we do get a little miffed with people who fail to recognise the seven-hundred-plus-year-old county of Lancashire in preference to a county that existed for only fourteen years.*'

Steve Sherdley kept up the pressure and told us about Lancashire Day. '*People have assumed that Lancashire places have "moved", so that Southport is now thought of as Merseyside, Hawkshead is thought of as Cumbrian, Wigan Greater Manchester and Warrington Cheshire, etc.*' The celebrations on 27 November remember 1295, when the first elected representatives of the county entered King Edward I's Model Parliament. Chris Dowson adds that red roses are worn and proclamations are read by town criers '*from the Furness Fells to the River Mersey, from the Irish Sea coast to the Pennines*'.

It is likely that administrative counties will be changed again as regions begin to assert their power and attempt to market themselves. It will fall to those who keep writing Middlesex on their letters, strong followings of friends, such as for Huntingdonshire, Lancashire and the smallest county for which we all have an underdog kind of fondness – Rutland – to demonstrate ways of maintaining their presence in the twenty-first century.

DAWN CHORUS

The sound of birds singing together at the break of day in spring is one of the wonders of the natural world. Many more sing then than at any other time of the day or year.

In the city the blackbird and robin may sing in the night, but in darker places either will wake the others before the sun rises. Birds in the South West begin their singing earlier in the year but easterly birds get up before them. The sun rises over Suffolk (Lowestoft, 05.15) 37 minutes before Cornwall (Penzance 05.52) on 4 May, where in 2003, in the Kensey valley outside Launceston, the sequence went as follows: robin (04.52), tawny owl (on his way to bed?), blackbird, pheasant, cockerel, wren (05.07 and getting light), blackcap, woodpigeon, jay, magpie, chaffinch, crow, mistle thrush, chiffchaff, great spotted woodpecker, green wood-pecker and finally blue tit and great tit (05.38). The robin sang for fifty minutes.

Apart from the joy of singing, it is observed that male birds are prob-ably establishing their territory and attracting a mate (the sedge warbler and the pied flycatcher stop singing after pairing). But why sing at dawn? Theories abound. Song, or rather lack of it, may reveal a vacant territory after a night death. In the cold of first light fewer insects are about, so why not warble?

Some places resound with more song than others. River birds sing less than birds of the woodland edge; the sedge warbler arriving from Africa in mid-April hardly draws breath before jazzing up its trills and rhythm changes. You will hear as much in Highgate and Queen's Woods, north London as you will in open farmland. And mature suburban gardens emulate woodland edge, so you may be able to lie in bed and have the best of both worlds. But effort will repay. A visit to a woodland before dawn breaks in May will impress both place and nature on the memory. On a dawn chorus walk at Leighton Moss, Lancashire you may hear the booming of the bittern; at Gibraltar Point, Lincolnshire you are more likely to hear the skylark, the 'peewit' of the lapwing or the incessant call of the cuckoo; on the Roundshaw Downs in the London borough of Sutton resound the songs of the whitethroat, blackcap and chiffchaff.

The chiffchaff calls its name, the wren hammers out 56 notes in 5.2 seconds, the chaffinch sings more than four hundred songs in an hour, the song thrush hones its song year by year by repeating each phrase three times. All in concert with greenfinch, goldfinch, dunnock, linnet, blackcap, willow warbler, blackbird, robin, pheasant, wood pigeon, blue tit and great tit.

In the city robin and blackbird dominate but the starling may sit on your balcony and, with feathers a-tremble, try out his mimicry – mobile phones have interested him recently. Research shows that traffic noise is taking its toll on birds, some not finding mates; the great tit is singing at higher frequencies among the sounds of the city just to be heard.

Anyone with a clear memory will recall rightly that the dawn chorus was much more intense a generation ago before we were assailed by the problems captured so vividly by Rachel Carson in *Silent Spring*. In March 1999 the Royal Society for the Protection of Birds reported that 27 million birds have simply vanished in a quarter of a century. We have four million fewer blackbirds, half the song thrushes and two-thirds of the mistle thrushes; linnets are down by one-third and yellowhammers by half. One of the reasons is loss of habitat; another is profligate use of pesticides and herbicides in garden and on farm. At this rate we shall be left with a little bit of bread and no birds.

DOG ROSES

The most common of our fourteen native wild roses, its root is said to have cured a soldier of the Praetorian Guard, who was bitten by a rabid dog, hence its name. *Rosa canina*'s scented single white or delicate pink flower and bright red hips are often out of reach, as it likes to climb high into the canopies of trees.

Wild roses may have been overshadowed by cultivated ones, but their very charm lies in finding them in the places where they want to grow. Wayside hedgerows and motorway verges in May and June are always enlivened by the elegant white/pink tangle.

The curator of the Cambridge Botanic Garden in the 1870s wrote: '*We all allow the Roses of the florist to be without rival among flowers of the garden, and we can but admit that wild Roses are perhaps the most lovely of flowers of the field. But there are numbers of the wildings, and all beautiful, and some of surpassing charm. We want to see them more often grown in our gardens.*'

Other wild roses of the hedgerows are the Burnet or Scotch rose – its creamy white, sweet-smelling flower is the first to open in May; the white-flowered field rose, smelling of honey; the pink-flowered downy rose, with soft, hairy leaves; and the sweet briar or Eglantine, which has a fragrant, deep pink flower and leaves that, when rubbed, smell of apples.

Crimson bedeguar galls formed by the larvae of the gall wasp, known as robin's pincushions, are often found on roses. Local names include robin redbreast's cushion in Sussex, briar boss in Shropshire, briar-ball in Northamptonshire and mossy gall in Wiltshire. They were used to cure whooping cough, toothache and rheumatism and as a charm to prevent flogging. It is difficult to believe that five hundred tons of rose hips were collected from hedgerows during 1943; the equivalent in vitamin C content to 25 million oranges.

The cultivated rose is often drawn upon as a symbol of England, but for many of us Rupert Brooke offered the truer spirit: '*unkempt about those hedges blows/An English unofficial rose*'.

DRAGONS

Stories help us to memorise and indeed visualise places. Cultures remaining closer to the land than ours tell stories to help find their way about, to know dangers, to know themselves and where they came from. Most dragon tales are geographically connected, sometimes to a roundish hill or mound, sometimes to water.

At Drakelow, the 'dragon's mound', in south Derbyshire, the reference is to a dragon protecting a treasure in a burial mound; the same story adhering to Wormelow Tump in Herefordshire reminds us that dragons were often referred to as worms. When the constellation of Draco (the dragon) dominated the sky, midsummer bonfires burnt bones to keep them at bay. With the Old English word for dragon being *draca*, there are also fields that carry memories: Drakestones in Stinchcombe, Gloucestershire; Drakelows in Thornton Hough, Cheshire.

Treasure-guarding stories carry echoes of Norse and Germanic myth. Thor attempts to destroy a vast serpent coiled about the whole world. In the great poem *Beowolf* the interwoven stories of Germanic tribes also involve a dragon roused by a thief. Seamus Heaney translates from the Anglo-Saxon:

> *The hoard guardian*
> *scorched the ground as he scoured and hunted*
> *for the trespasser who had troubled his sleep.*
> *Hot and savage, he kept circling and circling*
> *the outside of the mound.*

On the Yorkshire coast the waves crash and break against a ridge of flattish rocks; Heather Elvidge from Muston tells one story about how Filey Brigg came to be. A troublesome dragon in those parts made a hero out of Billy Biter, whose wife was eaten by the beast, followed by the parkin she had made. '*There was so much that its teeth became stuck together. So the dragon set off down the Ravine to the sea, where it began to wash the sticky stuff from its mouth ... Billy and his neighbours ... set up such a din with pots and pokers that the dragon was afraid to come ashore, so it had to stay in the sea, where it drowned ... it eventually turned to stone and it is still there to this day, stretching out into the sea.*'

Dragons, the devil and Satan seem interchangeable in old texts. '*Better to reign in hell than serve in heaven*' – Milton puts these words into the mouth of Satan as he leaves heaven with the Fallen Angels. Hell is a place of fire. The Bible (Revelation xii, 7-10) describes it thus: '*And there was war*

in Heaven: Michael and his angels fought against the dragon … And the great dragon was cast out, that old serpent, called the Devil, and Satan, which deceiveth the whole world.' Epstein's sculpture of St Michael on Coventry Cathedral has Satan beneath his feet; elsewhere, as at the church in St Bees, Cumberland, the dragon lies at his feet. Of the six hundred churches dedicated to St Michael, remarkable ones are found near or on rounded hills – Mere in Wiltshire, St Michael's Mount in Cornwall. Was the dragon already known there, or was he a construct of the new religion?

St George, of course, is England's champion dragon slayer; we share him as patron saint with Catalonia, Georgia, Greece, Lithuania, Palestine, Portugal, Genoa, Venice and more. A soldier turned evangelist, who died a terrible death in AD 303, his association with dragons appears in medieval times, when he saves a maiden from a dragon to gain thousands of souls for the Christian faith. His role locally is now more associated with socialising and quenching thirst, the George and Dragon being a favourite pub name.

Dragons also had a hard time from knights, prodigal sons and adventuring princes, who never gained sainthood. The best known is the Lambton Worm from Lambton Castle, County Durham.

Filey Brigg, Yorkshire.

Of the Knucker Hole near Lyminster, Sussex and its dragon, Jacqueline Simpson wrote: '*It is a pond locally reputed to be bottomless, though in fact it is about thirty feet deep, and it is fed from below by a strong underground source, so that it never freezes over, nor does the water level ever vary, even in an intense drought like that of 1976. At one time there were several such ... all known as "Knucker Holes" or "Nickery Holes" ... it is derived from an Anglo-Saxon word, nicor, which means "water monster" and occurs in Beowulf.*' The place-name, therefore, tells us that the story has been long in the telling. In a long and convoluted tale including much rampaging, a 'gert pudden' of flour and water seems to have played a part in the downfall of the Knucker.

Few of our dragons live to tell their own tales, so foul of mouth and habit they are portrayed, but the Chinese dragon, the Lung, is a noble, protective beast. It is particularly associated with rain, rivers and water-holes and brings good fortune. Two hundred dragons adorn the Chinese Archway in Liverpool, built to welcome the New Year of the Dragon in AD 2000. More dragons, always a symbol of power, stand guard at the entrance to Chinatown in Manchester on a Ming Dynasty Imperial Arch – each with feet of five talons. Commonplace dragons have only four.

DROVE ROADS

To this day painted on the Drover's House in Stockbridge, Hampshire, '*Gwair tymherus porfa flasus cwrw de a gwal cysurus*' offered to Welsh drovers good pasture, tasty beer and a cosy place to sleep. The driving of cattle, sheep, pigs and poultry by foot across long distances ended only with the coming of the railways in the nineteenth century. Drovers not only came from as far as Wales but also across the Cheviot Hills from Scotland.

They came along the Driving Road to Gearstones at Ribblehead, Cumberland. They came along the Maiden Way from Hadrian's Wall to Kirkby Thore, Westmorland, and down the Hambleton Drove between Durham and York. They dallied at the great trading fairs across Yorkshire and Lancashire and Horham St Faith in Norfolk, Chilham in Kent and Brentwood in Essex. The main destination was London's Smithfield and Cheapside markets. In 1600 around thirty thousand animals were being annually 'drifted' from Wales alone. The trade was already ancient: across East Anglia the Icknield Way's name preserves an old word for oxen, via the Iceni tribe, who lived along it.

Drovers brought news, gossip and money; the Black Ox was the symbol of one of their banks, later crucial in the development of Lloyds, the Ox evolving into the black horse. They have marked permanently the places through which they passed: Drover House, Northumberland; Sheephouse Barn and Guiting Power in Gloucestershire. Oxway, rothern, neat, droveden, shieling ... all speak of drovers.

In East Anglia droves were also called lokes. Across the country cattle might rest in halts, booths or lairages. Trespassing animals were held in a pinfold until errant drovers paid a fine. A field called Penny Piece or Halfpenny might be their night-time resting place, the name stating the price; Halfpenny Lane travels from the Berkshire Downs to Cholsey, Berkshire. Drover inns proliferated, such as the Drover's Rest at Monkhill, Cumberland and The Shepherd and Dog at Langham, Essex. The Bull and Last in Dartmouth Park, north London was the penultimate stop for northern drovers, perhaps referring to the last trough.

There are more physical reminders. Thirsk, Yorkshire has an old milestone showing a drover with his sheep. Lines of well-worn stemming stones are sometimes set into the ground across droves, 'traffic calming' measures for cattle hastening downhill. Forges lined the routes to make the crescent-shaped cattle shoes for the long walk. Yew trees marked the routes in Hampshire. A few Scots pines implied hospitality to Highland drovers.

DRYSTONE WALLS

Something of the identity of England is bound together by drystone walls: the hard work they betray, the geology they divulge, the patterns they make. They were built at different times in more than twenty, mostly upland, counties. Cornwall, Cumberland, Derbyshire, Westmorland and Yorkshire have more than half of the total, with the latter having the greatest length. The craft skills needed to make walls solid and safe, using no binding material, vary in time and place, as do the shapes of the fields enclosed. Together they reflect the way we have controlled the land, embodying a common wealth and an unwritten history often still awaiting translation.

Clearing the land of stones in order to work it challenged early settlers. Enclosure seems a by-product in West Penwith, where, at the furthest end of Cornwall, the density of drystone walls is at its greatest. Here, in the Iron Age and Romano-British times, enormous granite boulders, known as grounders, were built to and levelled off by smaller stones to make hundreds of small, irregular fields.

By contrast, straight walls made with quarried, flattish, hand-sized stones neatly mark out and show off the oolitic limestone swell of the Cotswolds. They were mostly created at the times of Parliamentary enclosure between 1760 and 1825. The rectilinear patterns suggest more recent enclosure of land, whereas sinuous walls tend to be very old.

Since their main task is to hold animals in or out, they need to be robust against climbing sheep, scratching cattle and pushing horses. Shelter against wind and snow also proves useful. Some were built to encircle mine shafts or to resolve ownership. The disputatious Yorkshire abbeys of Bolton, Fountains and Salley finally built walls along the Pennine tops in medieval times to mark their territories. Built and built again these still remind us of the early value of Malham Moor for sheep farming and mining.

Volcanic rock, Wasdale, Cumberland.

Cotswolds limestone, Sherborne estate,
Gloucestershire.

Dartmoor granite, Devon.

Millstone grit, Whaley Bridge, Derbyshire.

Geology offers or denies the possibility of stone walling. In lowland England the sudden appearance of walls instead of hedgerows or ditches usually gives away the underlying Jurassic limestone, as at North Rauceby in Lincolnshire, or volcanic intrusions, as in Leicestershire's Charnwood Forest, where hills are crossed by walls of dark boulders.

The culture of drystone walling is intricate. The county council in Cornwall specifies stone hedges where roads are widened, but there is an increasing tendency, even in western granite areas, to face them with cheaper northern slate, which is made to a herringbone pattern of 'Jack and Jills'. In Yorkshire the 'magpie' walls around the Craven Fault require a local touch.

The flavours are picked up in the words. Cripple holes allow the passage of sheep – they may go by the name of hogg holes or sheep creeps, smout holes or sheep smooses. Across Yorkshire the word used varies from lunkie, smoot and creep hole to thirl. Water smoots are built over simple stone lintels to allow streams to pass under them.

The walls of Wharfedale in Yorkshire are more simply built than those of Wensleydale, which have neat rows of through stones that protrude from each side. Dales sometimes developed their own style as roving gangs earned their living or followed specifications demanded by the Enclosure Awards.

In the High Peak of Derbyshire, whatever the geology, walls have three rows of through stones. Around Coniston in Lancashire and Ambleside in Westmorland solid slate is often used vertically, like gravestones standing shoulder to shoulder, to enclose the fields. In the Duddon valley at Far Kiln Bank you can look up to a nine-foot-high Cyclopean wall comprising huge boulders at its base finished by smaller ones.

At the other end of the country you can see through the seemingly haphazard walls that shamble across the Isles of Scilly. The ill-fitting angular granite is but a single stone deep; some islanders explain that this was to allow rapid removal and rebuilding if they had to launch or land boats in odd places because of a tempestuous sea.

The conditions of sun and shade, exposure and shelter on the opposing sides of walls make for interesting differences. Slate fences are hard and rather mean, except to lichens, but most walls attract lichens, ferns and mosses, stonecrop and saxifrage. Limestone flora is always richer, but the walls of the South West have warmth and longer days on their side. Cornish walls, found mainly on high ground, harbour wall penny-wort, stonecrop, wild thyme, polypody fern, spleenworts and dry stone mosses, yellow crustose and grey-green foliose lichens, dog's tooth lichen and more.

The imposing Cornish hedge bank, with its earth centre and battered stone facings, is often so profusely lived upon that it is hard to see the stones. Depending on exposure it offers a feast of plants: gorse, black-thorn, hawthorn, heather, bilberry, roses, Atlantic ivy, brambles and honeysuckle, and possibly oak, ash, elm, sycamore, holly, elder and hazel growing along the top. Among the concave stones, thrift, sea campion and kidney vetch might be found on the coast, or, inland, bluebell, red campion, foxglove, fumitory, hawkweeds, woundworts, common violet, toadflaxes and many more. Ferns might include hart's tongue, male fern, broad buckler, black spleenwort and soft shield fern. In Cumberland, where the river Ehen meets the sea south of St Bees Head, roughly stone-faced earth banks, called kefts, support gorse or hawthorn hedges.

Snails love all kinds of walls, as do spiders and glow-worms. The wall butterfly, like many of its fellows, enjoys soaking up solar energy on a warm wall. Small mammals, such as mice and voles, abound, so the adder, stoat, weasel and little owl find drystone walls perfect for hunting, as well as cover. Wheatear, perhaps intending to fly on to the Lake District, catch their breath on the Purbeck walls of Dorset. When they reach their summer grounds they will use the walls as highways, lookouts and feeding places. Walls make good nesting places for redstarts and spotted flycatchers, as well as wrens, blue tits, great tits and sparrows.

The ebb and flow of fortunes in farming has reached a giddy pitch during the past half-century. Ever bigger machinery demands wide access gates and turning circles, to the extent that many walls have been removed, the stone sold. Road construction and development eat away walls, while fashions in gardening provoke stealthy removal and sales. Neglect and clambering walkers bring further threat. A survey of the condition of drystone walls still standing in 1994 found that '*nearly half the country's walls were ruinous, derelict or not stockproof*'; a further 38 per cent were showing serious signs of advancing or potential deterioration. Nine per cent were stock-proof and just four per cent were in excellent condition. Out of seventy thousand miles, that does not amount to much.

EARTHWORKS

One story goes that Six Hills Barrows in Hertfordshire is the result of the devil pitching earth at Stevenage. Our forebears spent much creative energy explaining the works of those who went before. Now archaeology is revealing more and more about the subtle clues around us. Everywhere secretes its own stories; mundane rumples in the ground may prove the key to new understanding of a locality.

The more we know, the more we see the traces of activity of ancient peoples, often ploughed over or built upon so that we have overlooked the earth moved to make amphitheatres, banks, graves, barrows, camps, dykes, fish-ponds, fortifications, henges, mining pits and mounds, monumental hills, mottes, plague pits, ring ditches, salt workings and warrens. Nature may have reclaimed abandoned villages and remnants of farming and monastic activity, which show up when the shadows are long or drought dries out the ground.

It is difficult to miss the astonishing Silbury Hill, the largest constructed prehistoric mound in Europe. Built in the first half of the third millennium BC near Avebury in Wiltshire, it is contemporary with the early stages of Stonehenge and is thought to have had a ritual purpose.

More modest, Perran Round at Rose in Cornwall gives example to the richness of meaning gathered by these ancient places. Roger Glanville, part of the local history group that helped in its restoration, wrote in 1984 that it was '*originally constructed during the Iron Age as a fortified farm … During the Middle Ages the Round was adapted and used as a Plen an guary or open-air theatre for the enactment of Cornish miracle plays … the Round was used for many years as a preaching pit … as well as for children's Tea Treats and occasional village fêtes.*' It has also been used for Cornish

wrestling and for the Gorsedd of the Bards of Cornwall. By 2003 the Round was badly overgrown and the cycle of care and new use was beginning again.

EXMOOR PONIES

Around 21,000 years ago, with ice or tundra covering the country, the re-establishment of plants and animals had to wait until the permafrost receded. Some time during the succeeding oscillations of climate, colonisation by trees and the disappearance of the land bridge linking us to mainland Europe (between eight and five thousand years ago), a group of animals walked here and made themselves at home on the open moors that are the source of the Exe.

Isolated, the forebears of the Exmoor pony evolved and now persist as one of the world's most ancient breeds, somehow surviving man's predations and interferences. They are small, 11.2 to 13.1 hands high, with double-thickness coats that keep out the cold and wet. They are consistent in colour and marking – shades of brown with darker points and characteristic pale muzzle and eye surrounds. They are round, with extensive and efficient digestive systems carried on strong legs and feet that work well in wet and rocky conditions.

Exmoor, an exposed area of wild, high moorland on the border of Devon and Somerset, faces the winds of the Atlantic, which bring penetrating rain, snow and cold as well as hot, sunny days. From the eleventh century it was a royal forest – a hunting ground – but with no woods at all within its bounds. Any management of the ponies tended to be based upon the principle that nature had the best design and introducing other blood led to dilution of hardiness. But the moor was sold in 1818 to an industrialist bent on productivity. He bred the ponies to the extent that they could no longer survive the harsh conditions. Luckily the retiring Warden of the moor, Sir Thomas Acland, took thirty ponies and some of the surrounding farmers bought a few – to them we owe the continuance of the line. Many families are still breeding Exmoors and, on Winsford Hill, the descendants of Acland's herd are run, still carrying the Anchor brand mark.

The Second World War also nearly saw their end. Indiscriminate target practice and rustling for meat left barely fifty animals. Mary Etherington inspired other Exmoor farmers and they began a careful programme of breeding.

Only a small number of animals remain, with few bloodlines. So, although they are off the critical list, the Rare Breeds Survival Trust classes them as endangered. About two hundred feral Exmoor ponies still graze the moor, and across the world as few as twelve hundred exist. The Exmoor Pony Society oversees gatherings in October and November, where the year's youngsters are selected and branded. An annual stallion parade is held in Exford in early May.

Their continued presence on the moor is important; the place and the animal have evolved together for perhaps as long as there has been grass on Exmoor. They do not simply excite us as 'wild' creatures, they are, in some sense, the place itself. Full of stamina and strength, their lives were intertwined with those who made their living on the moor. They have been used for shepherding, driving, riding, agriculture and postal delivery.

But their future lies in finding new roles; in addition to tourism, driving and riding they are earning their keep in other ways. Although it means small, free-living herds working in other places, one promising task performed with relish is that of conserving grassland habitat, such as the Sussex Downs and Askham Bog in Yorkshire. Exmoors are very good at eating tough herbage – tor grass, thistles, invasive scrub – that crowds out delicate wildflowers. There is a positive symmetry in one highly endangered creature building its own survival on the saving of others.

FARMS & FARMSTEADS

There are lanes in Cornwall that take you on such intimate journeys through farmyards that you feel like an intruder. Scattered settlement characterises the South West and is discernible in Essex, the Weald of Kent and the Lake District. In the Somerset Levels and the Fens farms often clustered on islands of dry ground; in the North, around a defendable village green. Elsewhere people gathered cheek-by-jowl in villages, as in the Midlands, with gables to the street, surrounded by open fields, until enclosure came. Some old farmsteads may have occupied the same ground since Norman times and perhaps long before. The more we learn, the more longevity we read in the landscape. As people sought shelter, warmth and water, the buildings often seem to have grown out of the land, inclining, as H.J. Massingham would say, to the will of the geology.

Pastoral farming in the higher lands was always a lonelier task; farms in the Pennines and the Lakes are still isolated, although the collection of buildings may give them the air of a tiny hamlet. Elsewhere isolation usually tells of assarting – the clearing of woodland or moor – survival of pestilence, or enclosure.

Much rebuilding dates from 1570 to 1640, a little later in the North, as economic prosperity and European fashion drove changes from the wealthier South East. While these traditional buildings may have been superseded, many still populate their land with confidence: the granite long houses stepping down Dartmoor slopes (with house at the top end, a cross passage and animals on the down side); the Peak Forest laithe houses, with barn and byre all under the same roof; the fortified farmhouses of Cornwall; and bastles, with living quarters above animals, built for defence along the Scottish border.

It is unusual in the East and South East to find the house attached to the farm buildings. The Yorkshire Dales are populated with field barns, called laithes, far from the village farmhouses. Where the buildings are separate there are still examples in Lancashire of barns combining cow house and threshing space, and bank barns making use of slopes. The working buildings tend to remain unadorned and might be gathered around a courtyard, be built in parallel, make a U or L shape, or have been organically collected over time.

Perhaps a third of farms disappeared in the late eighteenth century. Old buildings became workers' cottages or smallholdings, and in the areas of enclosure from the Midlands to Dorset between 1750 and 1850 dispersed farms were built in the middle of new holdings. Model farms were established by the bigger landlords during the eighteenth and nineteenth centuries to demonstrate evolving good practice. Quadrangles, paved yards and octagonal dairies brought a new formality, and in the early twentieth century model farms developed hygiene practices and mechanisation. Farms that were hitherto mixed began to separate out, with dairying, beef and sheep concentrated in the wetter West and the hills, and the East and South growing more grain.

English Heritage says that '*Traditional farm buildings are by far the most numerous type of historic structure in the countryside.*' Many have been adapted to new uses or saved by corrugated iron. To the distinctive combinations of farmhouse, barns, work sheds, animal houses and hemmel

Laithe house, near Todmorden, Yorkshire.

or linhay (open-fronted cattle shelters), the last century has added the Dutch barn, silo, silage pit and drying kiln, all homogenising in their large scale, materials and ubiquitous colours. Old buildings ill-fitted to modern use have been replaced or converted into workshops or homes. Many farmers have found sale with planning permission a way of supporting farm income, and the coherence of the farmyard has been lost.

Where it persists, the integrity of the farmstead remains one of the touchstones of local distinctiveness. The whitewashed farmhouse of Lakeland is rare to see in bare-stone north Yorkshire; the black-and-white, timber-rich buildings of Shropshire, bricks of Nottinghamshire, weather-board in Kent and white- or pink-painted cob in Devon reflect and create the vernacular, together with the disposition of the buildings. As English Heritage says, '*the historic farm buildings of the countryside present a particularly acute dilemma … large-scale dereliction of buildings or, equally, the wholesale, poorly informed or ill-conceived conversion of surplus buildings could irrevocably damage important and irreplaceable historic assets … impair valued landscapes and damage their appeal for locals and visitors.*'

Devonshire long house, near Widecombe in the Moor, Devon.

Yet they need a function to survive, and so do farmers. The number of holdings is fast diminishing and with them much knowledge. Farms should not be factories, they are the unique and varied expression of long relationships with the land. Farming by GPS has nothing to do with wisdom, and much of value to the locality is lost as global practice and economics override familiarity.

Farming for local consumption can, on the other hand, reinforce direct contact with the surrounding community, decrease remoteness, spread knowledge, understanding and responsibility and bring environmental and welfare benefits, since transport is minimised. As European grant systems change from supporting production to encouraging conservation, there may be a chance for local distinctiveness to re-assert itself.

FERRIES

The ferryman at Symonds Yat, Herefordshire pulls the punt across the Wye by rope. Tiring but effective in quiet waters, this is one step up from the simple rowing boat that crosses the river Blyth from Walberswick to Southwold in Suffolk. One of the several ferries that crossed the Severn in Shropshire survives at Hampton Loade, its name recalling the Old English for ford or river crossing. It is a two-minute, fifty-pence journey, joining the east and west banks and the cottages beside them. The small wooden passenger ferry is moved or restrained by pulley along a chain, the ferryman or -woman using the rudder to make it move sideways across the river. It was threatened with closure, but a grant has not only ensured its survival, but created a new boat, maintaining an important link for residents, cyclists and walkers.

Rivers unite and divide; many used to be highways. The river Derwent, which marks the boundary between east and west Yorkshire, was once criss-crossed by small ferries, many run by farms and cottages on a request

basis. Clues abound, such as tracks or footpaths leading to the water's edge, and pubs at the end of lanes with rivers as their only neighbours.

Car ferries add an extra dimension to a journey and give one a chance to savour the place. In Norfolk a small, brightly coloured car ferry crosses the river Yare at Reedham, linking both sides of the B1140. Pull's ferry operates on the river Wensum in Norwich; James Pull spent 46 years as ferryman here in the nineteenth century. The village of Bawdsey Manor on the river Deben in Norfolk is linked to Felixstowe by ferry across the estuary in summer. In Cornwall the road drops steeply down beside Daphne du Maurier's old house to the ferry, which travels every day of the week across the ria from the village of Bodinnick to Fowey, allowing cars to avoid a twelve-mile detour via the nearest bridge at Lostwithiel. Fowey is also linked to the 'other side' by a small motorised passenger ferry, which goes to the village of Polruan.

Only some large river crossings have been replaced by road links, such as the great Severn and Humber bridges. The latter is a couple of miles downstream from where the Romans embarked and disembarked, at Winteringham on the south side and Brough (Petuaria) on the north side of the estuary.

Some stretches of water retain their boat crossings in places where high-clearance bridges would be needed to allow large ships to enter the docks. At Poole harbour in Dorset the ferry runs along underwater cables across the demandingly tidal Swash Channel between the two sandy peninsulas of Sandbanks and Shell Bay. Any perched herring gull is always called Charlie, and the resident ghost of a former skipper is said to switch lights on and off, although the *Bramble Bush Bay* is the fourth ferry to date.

Gosport ferry, Portsmouth harbour, Hampshire.

In slowing us down ferries remind us what formidable barriers rivers and tidal waters can be, and they help to accentuate the differences between one side and the other. 'Ferry 'cross the Mersey' is still a familiar sight. Two passenger services link Liverpool and the Wirral peninsula, although cars use two tunnels – the Kingsway and the Queensway; the latter's completion in 1934 was celebrated with a walk-through of eighty thousand people. A ferry has crossed the Tyne between North and South Shields since at least 1377, and the two present ferries continue every half-hour – the *Pride of the Tyne* was built at the Swan Hunter yard in its last

Fowey to Bodinnick ferry, river Fowey, Cornwall.

years. Yellow passenger ferries bustle around in Bristol, including the *Independence*, a shallow-draughted launch that once took passengers ashore from ships in the Severn.

The longest ferry journey in England is from Penzance in Cornwall to the Isles of Scilly. It takes two hours and forty minutes, making it further than some of the services from the Kent ports to mainland Europe. Walkers on the South West Coast Path join locals at St Mawes in Cornwall, where a small ferry crosses to St Anthony Head in Falmouth Bay, and at the South Hams in Devon, where foot passengers can cross the river Yealm between Noss Mayo, Newton Ferrers and Warren Point. Another boat crosses the Avon from Bantham slipway to Cockleridge Ham.

These small excitements are much preferable to the extended car-park experiences of the cross-Channel services. But the many ferries that still work provide more than pleasure: without them the plashy places and islands would have fewer visitors and little cargo, and many river communities would be parted by water.

FIELD PATTERNS

In north Cornwall, where the parishes of St Ives and St Just meet the sea, as many as two hundred fields to the square kilometre betray a rugged landscape long worked. In East Anglia it is possible to find lands unfenced to the far horizon.

Dark shadows striate a hillside, simple terraces reminiscent of a Mediterranean vineyard but grazed by cattle or sheep. Strip lynchets, like dry, grassy cascades, dominate groups of hillside fields from Wharfedale in Yorkshire to the cliffs at Worth Matravers in Dorset.

Near Malham, Yorkshire.

The treads and risers of these flamboyant staircases originate from medieval times, but in some places lynchets mark prehistoric farming.

Side by side, or one on top of the other, field patterns date from different periods yet jostle on the stage we inhabit today. Fields are living history, cultural landscapes to be read. Farmers first worked some of them four thousand years ago and, although many are disappearing under development and deep ploughing, the patterns await deciphering.

> So they drained it long and crossways in the lavish Roman style –
> Still we find among the river-drift their flakes of ancient tile,
> And in drouthy middle August, when the bones of meadows show,
> We can trace the lines they followed sixteen hundred years ago.

RUDYARD KIPLING, from 'The Land'

Relict Roman fields are rare, but on the silt lands of the Fens around March in Cambridgeshire and on Martin Down in Hampshire the bones are visible.

A wide stripe from Dorset to Durham, Sussex to Norfolk, known by agricultural historians as the Central Province, was dominated by huge open fields created in medieval times, each tended strip by strip. In Braunton in Devon, Haxey in Lincolnshire, Soham in Cambridgeshire and at the tip of the Isle of Portland in Dorset, vestiges of the great open fields can be seen. At Laxton in north Nottinghamshire there is a fascinating survival of the system, although the undulations of ridge-and-furrow strips have long been ploughed flat.

This swathe of country is now the landscape of enclosure, which brought dramatic change to the look, feel and working of the land. Common fields were taken in by landholders during a century of Acts of Parliament gathering pace from 1750. These shadowed agricultural reform, imprisoning more and more land behind fences and hedges, to be farmed scientifically using new equipment and grazed by selectively bred cattle and sheep. The Enclosures brought *'large nucleated settlements and distinctive field systems, in sharp contrast to other parts of England where much older enclosed field systems and dispersed patterns of farmstead and hamlet form the historical character of the landscape'*, David Hall writes. Typically geometry dominates, with regular squarish fields, wide-verged straight and dog-leg roads and angular hedges – formal, but not as elegant as the Georgian houses that were appearing at the same time. The manifold losses were mourned by John Clare in his native Northamptonshire:

> *Inclosure came and trampled on the grave*
> *Of labour's rights and left the poor a slave …*
> *Fence now meets fence in owners' little bounds*
> *Of field and meadow large as garden grounds*
> *In little parcels little minds to please*
> *With men and flocks imprisoned ill at ease*

JOHN CLARE, from 'The Mores'

Illegal enclosure and squatting also saw the erosion of much common land. In Dorset heathland was being bounded by banks and, just to the north in the Blackmore Vale, twenty Acts of Parliament legitimised the enclosure and removal of woodland. In Lancashire, Chat Moss was drained and made into fields, as was much of the Somerset Levels and the Fens.

The word 'field' implies containment, and their shapes have given the landscape enthusiast much to explore. Christopher Taylor summarised: *'In Devon we find small irregularly shaped fields bounded by large banks, which are often surmounted by huge thick hedges. In Sussex the rolling downlands are a sea of arable land, divided occasionally by wire-mesh fences. Over much of the east Midlands the most common types of fields are those of rigidly geometric form defined by hedges, largely of hawthorn, with occasional trees. Over the fenlands of eastern England there is an infinite variety of field shapes and sizes, each bounded by narrow and usually straight drainage ditches. Farther north in Westmorland and Cumberland the small stone-walled paddocks, or strip-shaped fields on the sides of the dales, give way to vast areas delineated by apparently endless walls.'*

Reading the fields demands an eye for superimposition, a nose for tracing layer upon layer of activity, and not only in the countryside. Christchurch Meadow still hangs in the middle of Oxford, but every city and town carries some memory of *The Fields Beneath*, Gillian Tindall's evocative title for an exploration of the history of Kentish Town in north London. She shows the old field boundaries predisposing housing expansion to follow street by street.

Since the Second World War and our entry into the European Union, fields have grown to accommodate big machines and escalating economic expectations. Stone walls and hedges have been removed, sadly not liberating the land as Clare might have wished, but rendering it less readable, less rich in nature and less welcoming.

FOOTBRIDGES

Thomas Hardy in *The Mayor of Casterbridge* describes that moment of contemplation above the middle of a stream: '*These bridges had speaking countenances. Every projection in each was worn down to obtuseness partly ... by friction from generations of loungers, whose toes and heels had from year to year made restless movements against these parapets, as they stood there meditating on the aspects of affairs.*' The river Frome takes a gentle swing around Dorchester (Caster-bridge), and many little bridges cross it. Further downstream at Moreton the river is shallow and wide – an old fording place. The hundred-yard-long bridge isn't particularly attractive, made of concrete with metal rails,

Colber Bridge, river Stour, Sturminster Newton, Dorset.

but the setting lends it magic. You can see the tiny fry gathering around the piers and darting off like shape-shifting clouds as a horse and rider lazily amble across the ford. In the adjoining catchment of the Stour, the stone-piered Colber Bridge at Sturminster Newton has simple horizontal iron railings, while between Canford and Wimborne the footpath crosses the river by a narrow but sophisticated suspension bridge.

Where shallow streams run beside roads through sleepy villages, small footbridges have been built for access. Often they are straightforward beam bridges of stone or single arches, but in Mere, Wiltshire, where a row of gardens backs onto the shallow Shreen Water, bridge after bridge has its own personality; some have elaborate railings with cross bracing. At Otterton in Devon simple flat stones lie on beams to link roadway with footpath and houses. Packhorse bridges and bridges beside fords (known as clams in the South West) have found a lasting use by walkers; in Milldale, Derbyshire, a stone bridge sturdily spans the river Dove.

The celebrated Millennium Bridge over the Tyne in Newcastle is one of a new generation of urban footbridges. Opened in 2001, the newest of seven, the 'Blinking Eye' is the world's first tilting bridge. To let ships pass underneath the entire structure pivots 45 degrees to form a gateway fifty metres high. Each opening and closing takes just four minutes; it is so finely balanced that the energy required costs £3.60. Designed by Wilkinson Eyre Architects for Gateshead council, this is the only purpose-built bridge for pedestrians and cyclists across the Tyne (it links two cross-country riverside cycle ways), and the first opening bridge to be built across the Tyne for a hundred years.

The 'Blinking Eye', river Tyne, Gateshead.

FOOTPATHS

The path is the oldest mark we ever made upon the land, history written in a single line. A link with all the feet that have trodden there gives significance to all those tracks that strike out across moors, linking village with village and valley with valley – lanes for coffins, smugglers, lovers, pilgrims, salt traders, drovers, lead and stone carriers, school-children and churchgoers.

Our pattern of footpaths both illustrates and symbolises rights of passage created by generations of ordinary people going about their business. That they are to be cherished simply for their commonplace qualities and because they are everywhere may seem odd, but the intricate network of paths provides a vital link with the land. The path was born long before land was 'owned'.

A route 'padded' down by frequent use became, in the Anglo-Saxon tongue, a *paeth*. Morpeth in Northumberland means, sombrely, 'murder path'. Northern England has a colourful litany of words for paths, especially those going up hills: bar, bargh, borstal, bostal, burstel, peth. Bostel crops up in Sussex, too. Norfolk might instead have a loke. Derbyshire paths can be racks, as at Wreakes Lane in Dronfield. The Bonsall Parish Map shows paved paths criss-crossing the fields to link different parts of the village with each other, connecting one squeeze stile to another.

Around Strelley and Cossall in Nottingham-shire remnants of stone causeways known as monks' or pilgrims' paths may be part of the four-teenth-century monastic trade network. In the Fens people hardly left footprints; they used poles to vault ditches – in Friesland, Holland this is still a springtime sport. In Lancashire and Yorkshire the laborious and heavy work that went into

Plymouth, Devon.

making packhorse ways has left us with beautiful slabs, causeys, stone trods or flag paths. These routes, worn down by two to three hundred years of packhorse hooves, now enable dry walking, for example across the moors above Slack and Heptonstall.

The Countryside Agency suggests we have 120,000 miles of public rights of way. But walking along a 'right of way' is different from striking out across country. There have been tensions at every turn. John Ruskin wrote in 1885 to the *Pall Mall Gazette*: '*Sir – Will you kindly help me to direct general attention to the mischief now continually done by new landowners in the closing of our mountain footpaths? ... Of all the small, mean, and wicked things a landlord can do, shutting his footpath is the nastiest.*' Ewan MacColl recalls a time in the aftermath of the Industrial Revolution when weekly the people of the northern cities broke free from the looms, steelworks and mines:

> *I'm a rambler, I'm a rambler, from Manchester way*
> *I get all my pleasure the hard, moorland way.*
> *I may be a wage slave on Monday,*
> *But I am a free man on Sunday ...*

From 'The Manchester Rambler'

It was on a Sunday that the Kinder Scout Mass Trespass took place, on 24 April 1932. This brave gathering of hundreds of people from Manchester and Sheffield on the 2,088-foot peak in Derbyshire, despite the presence of gamekeepers who lined up to stop them, was a high point in the movement towards broad access to open country that is only now being achieved. The Hayfield and Kinder Scout Ancient Footpaths Association had sought a 'right to roam' since 1876. After the original trespass, ten thousand people assembled in the nearby Winnats Pass, an ancient salt way, for rallies to support the creation of national parks. Out of these actions came the Peak District National Park in 1951, the first of many, and, after persistent work by the Ramblers' Association and others, the Countryside and Rights of Way Act in 2000.

New recreational paths have to be mapped out and negotiated, linking old and new rights of way. It is not an easy task. Creating a right of way along the route of Hadrian's Wall demanded sensitive discussion with seven hundred landholders, many highly sceptical of the notion of access for all. Farmers and archaeologists imagined disturbance and loss. It took nearly twenty years to traverse the legal and diplomatic minefield: Hadrian's Wall Path was opened in 2003 with many new stiles, fourteen new footbridges – some in the weathered steel of industrial Tyneside – and turf protection for ancient buildings. A march along this now civil path might take three days in two-thousand-year-old footprints along the 84 miles from Wallsend, Northumberland to the Firth of Solway, Cumberland.

Disused railway lines and river and canal towpaths, where open, provide easy access for the wheelchair-bound and pram pushers – the Tissington Trail following the old Ashbourne to Buxton line in Derbyshire has thirteen miles of flat walking. The real heroes of countryside and town are the unsung paths, the twitchels, dog walks and ambling ways. But problems still abound – perhaps a third of footpaths are obstructed by barbed wire, broken bridges or padlocked gates.

Quaker's Causeway, near Guisborough, Yorkshire.

Herefordshire is rich in footpaths; Lincolnshire has far fewer. This may be a result of extensive as opposed to intensive farming and the loss of hedgerows, but it must also reflect the power of large landowners in the East. An area full of footpaths is in part a memorial to the hard work of local people to keep the rights alive.

GATES

The wooden field gate, with its gateposts and detail, offers a small working text of vernacular engineering, with a long history and a previously insistent geography. The demanding alternative in woodless parts, still in use on the Isles of Scilly, is to fill up the hole with piled stones and remove them every time you need access.

In the gritstone of the Forest of Bowland in Lancashire the gate 'stoops' and wall copings are carved with sophisticated parallel grooves. At Appleton-le-Moors in Yorkshire dark balls on the tops of the gateposts are known locally as the devil's eyes. Sturdy gateposts of red sandstone guard the fields of the Carndurnock peninsula in Cumberland. In the mountains of Borrowdale, Cumberland you may see the remains of tall, slender slate posts, with five or six holes through which poles could be fitted. In Yorkshire, in the Dales and around Halifax, slip gates worked on a similar principle – on one side of the gap the stone posts have holes, on the opposite side inverted L-shaped slots. In Nidderdale they are called stang stoops.

One simple and effective form of hinging to make a gate swing open and closed can still be seen occasionally in the walls of Westmorland and Cumberland. The vertical pole of the gate sits in holed stones, top and bottom, enabling it to turn; slate makes it easy. Some have traced this method to the Etruscans and Egyptians. In 1898 Joseph Wright followed this ancient hinging method in the words har, harl, haur, haw and her, through Scotland, Northumberland, Durham, Cumberland, Yorkshire

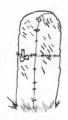

Solway coast, Cumberland.

Forest of Bowland, Lancashire.

Castleton, Derbyshire.

Tamar valley, Cornwall.

and Lancashire and as far south as Somerset, Wiltshire and Hampshire. The heavy hinge-end vertical is still often called the arle-, arr-, hartree-, hur- or harr-end of the gate. So dialect remains a conduit of culture as much as the gates themselves; our history follows us in words as well as artefacts.

Gates with bars closer together near the ground tell of sheep and lambs, sturdy higher gates of cattle and horses. They had to be strong and were made to last sixty to a hundred years. Oak is still the favoured wood, combining durability with lightness, followed by ash, Scots pine or larch, depending on locality. Cleft oak gates must have been common and they persist in oak-rich counties, such as Sussex, but mostly the less durable sawn oak has beaten its forebear in popularity for ease of making. In the Weald of Kent and Sussex, sweet chestnut is much used.

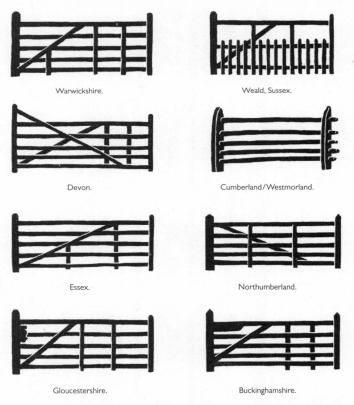

Warwickshire.

Weald, Sussex.

Devon.

Cumberland/Westmorland.

Essex.

Northumberland.

Gloucestershire.

Buckinghamshire.

The Sussex heave-gate is a simple cleft oak or chestnut lift gate with a diminutive fence of verticals along the bottom. Hazel hurdles are sometimes still used to fill a gap.

We can speculate that gates, like hedges and walls, had been perfected locally over hundreds of years. The gate pattern that now predominates usually has five bars, closer together at the bottom, and is braced by a wide V crossed by an inverted V. Some claim an Oxfordshire beginning, some believe it originated in East Anglia. In Devon and parts of Cornwall gates have perhaps five or six bars, two verticals and a diagonal brace from the top bar at the harr-end to the bottom of the first vertical. Most have tall harr-ends with the brace starting high above the top bar. In Berkshire, Surrey and Buckinghamshire you may see gates that have a top bar thickened at the harr-end, with a brace that flies diagonally up from the bottom of the harr-end.

Gloucestershire gates had beautifully carved harr-ends and elegant ironwork. Much pride went into their making – they were to be read by your great-grandchildren, after all. Anthea Brian reports that initials and dates have been found discreetly carved into the hinge sides of estate gates in her part of Herefordshire. In the nineteenth century overlarge O, W and M were used more as brand than brace. Y for Yeatman is still in use throughout the estate at Stock Gaylard in Dorset, more interesting for the fact that 'gyeat' is how the locals would say 'gate', as in William Barnes's poem 'The geate a-vallen to' – straight from the Old English *geat*. Names such as Yate, Yately, Woodyates, Donyatt and Leziate all suggest gate. Gate itself may mean 'gate', unless its root is Danish, as in York and Nottingham, where it means 'street'.

There is resurgent interest in the particularity of gate patterns. After all, this is a subtle way to tell people where they are. Common Ground has tried to persuade landowning agencies, such as the Forestry Commission and local authorities, to research, encourage and commission local patterns. We want to be able to say, with Moreland: '*In some parts of the country it would be possible to locate oneself pretty exactly by a study of the design of local gates.*'

Once you have noticed these small signatures, you cannot help looking in the hope that particularity and local knowledge, woodland and jobs are still tied together through this simplest of forms. It is clear from the range of gates still being made that it is possible to achieve standards without standardisation.

GLOW-WORMS

'*The Gloworm is a sort of catterpillar insect,*' John Clare explained in the early to mid-1800s, '*and thousands of them may be seen on Casterton Cowpasture on a summer night they appear as if a drop of dew hung at their tails which had been set on fire by the fairys for the purpose of a lanthorn.*' No such concentrations of glow-worms exist now anywhere in England, never mind just down the lane in Northamptonshire.

As with the flash of the kingfisher, you always remember where you have seen glow-worms. And an evening walk on a moonless, warm summer evening has one scanning the edge of tall grass and springy downland turf, hedge bottom along the lanes or disused railway lines, for the pinpricks of pale greenish light. These magical little signals from female glow-worms, actually small flightless beetles that look like grubs, are searchlights for males, who take flight after dark in search of mates. The light is a kind of bioluminescence, produced by a chain of chemical reactions and emitted from the last three segments of the female's body.

After mating the female lays her '*pale luminous yellow*' eggs, as John Tyler described them, on the undersides of leaves and on grass stems, then dies. Adults live only for two or so weeks; the bulk of their lives, about three years, is spent as larvae, sucking the juices from small slugs and snails.

Glow-worms are now mainly found in southern England and on the chalk, where snails are most numerous, although they do occur in other parts of the country. They appear to be declining, probably because of the destruction of their habitat and difficulty of the flightless female to colonise new areas. But an additional problem could be the proliferation of street lighting, which may prevent the male from seeing the female's glow.

For the past few years glow-worm walks have been organised by wildlife groups and the National Trust. In 1991 a colony of glow-worms was saved from destruction by the laying of a gas pipeline in Barrowden, Rutland. Villagers negotiated the re-routing of the pipeline around the glow-worms' hedgerow home.

GREEN LANES

Green lanes, unmetalled tracks, have somehow escaped the changes demanded by motor transport. Owned by many different farmers and landholders, some are just wide enough for a cart; others, fifty feet wide, are bounded by banks, hedges, ditches or drystone walls. They include ancient tracks and more recent unmade roads. The Ridgeway, running from Dorset to the Chilterns, and other ridgeways of the chalk country often follow watersheds. Some are tellingly known as summerways.

'*Every lane has its history,*' W.G. Hoskins wrote. '*It is not there by accident, and every twist it makes once had some historical meaning which we can decipher today, but not often.*' Tracks from the coast, some for carrying exotic contraband; routes for moving livestock or droving to markets near and far; roads for miners, traders and soldiers; paths between abbeys and pilgrims' ways: all tell stories within the landscape. In the northern Pennines they may still be called thrufts; in Lincolnshire gatterams.

Grundles suggest a gravelled surface, common in East Anglia.

The passage of animals to market, some walking from Scotland or Cornwall to London, is suggested by halfpenny and farthing fields (where stock could be kept overnight), inns called the Drover's or the Shepherd's Rest, or a handful of Scots pines on the horizon. Parts of long-distance routes, such as the Ridgeway and Icknield Way, have

Horton Scar Lane, Ribblesdale, Yorkshire.

large sections that are unmetalled. Valerie Belsey described the situation, when timber, for example, was hauled very simply without wheels: '*The resulting erosion ... by the sledges led these primitive hauliers to create parallel tracks, such as on the Icknield Way at Goring.*'

An old packhorse route over Salter Fell in the Forest of Bowland, Lancashire was hailed by Alfred Wainwright as '*possibly the finest moorland walk in England*'. Salt, the great preserver of meat and fish, was transported far and wide by lines of laden horses. From the seventeenth century, from the underground sources in Cheshire, Staffordshire and Worcestershire, salt ways fanned out from Nantwich, Northwich, Middlewich, Baswich, Shirleywich and Droitwich. Some can be located by names, such as Salters fords, lanes and bridges. The suffix 'wich' had taken on the implied meaning of brine workings in the Dark Ages.

Trackways crossed the Lincolnshire Wolds east–west to take salt inland. Long before the mining of rock salt and the Roman roads that enabled quicker distribution, salt had been evaporated from sea water all around the coast, in some cases for thousands of years. Middle and late Bronze-Age salt production has been found at Fenn Creek by South Woodham Ferrers and Mucking in Essex, and the names Eastwick, Bridgewick and Landwick also suggest old workings. The turf causeways from the sea's edge across the Essex marshes are raised slightly above the surrounding land; many link the 'red hills' – grassy mounds that are relics of salt evaporation methods – enabling sheep to get to higher ground at the highest tides.

In south Devon the medieval system of tracks was even more intricate than today's roads. Abbots Way links abbeys on the south and west of Dartmoor, but many connect moor with coast, offering breathtaking views of the sea. A survey by Valerie Belsey, begun in 1983, identified 191 green lanes covering 450 miles of the county, many overgrown and unlinked. South Hams district council has begun restoration, with the help of landholders and volunteers. A deeply incised and wooded lane near Mothecombe is not untypical, but often they are more open, with high hedge banks and grassy tracks that are excellent for wildflowers, birds and butterflies.

Walkers share these quiet lanes, not only with infrequent and indigenous farm traffic but also with cyclists, horse riders and, increasingly, motorbikes and four-by-four vehicles, claiming 'once a highway always a highway'. Some of the lanes are even more churned up than they would have been after bad weather and hundreds of cattle in the early nineteenth century. The impact and conflict in some lanes of the Yorkshire Dales, Lake District and Hampshire has led to vehicles being experimentally banned. David Gardiner, while chairman of the Green Lanes Environmental Action Movement, observed: '*The condition of the Ridgeway is nothing short of a disgrace and it's getting worse and worse so it is no longer a pleasure to walk. This ancient road is up to six thousand years old. It is surrounded by ancient monuments but I have seen four-by-fours using an Iron Age burial mound as a ramp to perform stunts.*'

GREETINGS

'Aye up, mi duck.' In Nottinghamshire and Derbyshire local people rarely say 'hello' or 'hi'. 'Aye up, yowth' and occasionally still 'Aye up, serry' (possibly from sirrah) are also heard, and there is a version of 'how are you' or 'how do you do' – 'Aa do?' – that may be accompanied by a tick of the head to the side. Sometimes just the action suffices. 'Awreet, mon?' (Newcastle), 'Ah do' or 'Ow do' (North and West), 'Ow bis?' (West) and 'Oroyt, moyte' (Birmingham) all suggest a question, but do not necessarily expect an answer, save the same: 'alright'.

Tom Rawling captures the rhythm in his poem 'The Old Showfield', recalling the Ennerdale Show in Cumberland. '*"How do?", "How ista?", "What's thi fettle?",/"Champion", "Middlin", "Nut sa Bad".*'

Cockneys were saying 'wotcher' in the sixteenth century – what cheer? Possibly this came with coals from Newcastle, where they still say 'Whaat cheor?' as well as 'Hulloo, hinnie', pet or petal. 'Ello, my dear' takes over in the West Country, and further south west 'Ello, my lover', contrasting with 'Yo' in Brixton and 'Wassup' in Caribbean/city/youth slang. East Enders might call you cock, cobber, chum, darlin', dear, guvna, luv, mate; in the eastern counties it might be bor. It all depends on who you are speaking to and your intimacy with them.

HARES

> The hare, the hare-kin,
> Old Big-bum, Old Bouchart,
> The hare-ling, the frisky one,
> Old turpin, the fast traveller,
> The way-beater, the white-spotted one,
> The lurker in ditches, the filthy beast,
> Old Wimount, the coward,
> The slinker-away, the nibbler
> The one it's bad luck to meet, the white-livered,
> The scutter, the fellow in the dew,
> The grass nibbler, Old Goibert,
> The one who doesn't go straight home, the traitor,
> The friendless one, the cat of the wood…
> The hare's mazes…
> The dew-beater, the dew-hopper,
> The sitter on its form, the hopper in the grass…
> The stag of the cabbages, the cropper of herbage…
> The animal that all men scorn,
> The animal that no one dares name…

This is but the start of a list of 'Names of the Hare in English', a late thirteenth-century poem from Shropshire. It offers 77 different names for the hare, many of them derogatory, supposedly for the hunter to recite. The hare was one of the taboo animals of ancient Britain; even her name (many thought all were female) should not be spoken, hence the alternatives.

The mountain hare is native. While some believe that the brown hare has been here since the Iron Age, it is more likely that it was brought here two thousand years ago and has pushed the mountain hare into the hills.

Hares were believed to bring good and bad luck: if a fisherman in the North East met one on the way to work, he went home. Elsewhere to encounter one may be lucky, unless it is white. In Cornwall a white hare presaged storms.

The hare was a symbol of spring's fertility in ancient Egypt and later in Europe as well, where it became associated with the goddess Eostre and, more recently, with Easter customs. An old game was to search for eggs laid by the Easter Hare, which became displaced by North America's preference for the Easter Bunny.

George Ewart Evans and David Thomson's exposition *The Leaping Hare* says: '*a Claydon (Suffolk) woman told us she used to say Hares, Hares before going to bed on the last day of the month, and Rabbits, Rabbits, when she got up in the morning. But this is a very common custom. The connection of the hare with the moon and therefore with the monthly cycle needs no further comment.*' Many legends and rich folklore link the hare with the moon, the supernatural, fertility, spring, fire and witches. It was commonly held that witches would transform themselves into hares.

The number of hares shot on farms and by organised drives on estates, usually in February, was estimated at two to three hundred thousand per year by the Burns Report in 2000. Once widespread, hares have declined in numbers since the 1960s, owing to the intensification of farming, increased use of agrichemicals and the move from cutting hay to earlier silage – the cutters kill the leverets, which stay in their forms (nests) among the growing crop. Hares are now most likely to be seen on the arable farms of Cambridgeshire, Norfolk and Suffolk or on aerodromes. They are taken by foxes and buzzards and poached by gangs of men with lurchers.

Hares can be differentiated from rabbits by their larger size, extraordinary amber eyes, longer ears with black tips and large, powerful hind legs. They can reach speeds of 45 miles per hour over short distances and can change direction suddenly, which helps them to evade predators – this is called the maze. This agility has been both their saving and their downfall: man has enjoyed the spectacle of pitting dogs against hares for sport. Before the Hunting Act 2004 made it illegal, hares were hunted by one hundred packs of beagles, basset hounds (on foot) and harriers (on horseback) and by about 24 hare-coursing clubs (using greyhounds and whippets). The annual Waterloo Cup at Great Altcar, near Southport, Lancashire, a three-day hare-coursing event, attracted ten thousand spectators in 2003.

Lines from William Blake's 'Auguries of Innocence' are brought to mind – '*Each outcry of the hunted hare/A fibre of the brain does tear*' – and from *The Dog Beneath the Skin* by W.H. Auden: '*Happy the hare at morning, for she cannot read/The Hunter's waking thoughts…*'

The hare's unusually gregarious springtime behaviour of chasing and 'fighting' is a ritual of the mating season. A dominant male (buck or jack) will chase and drive away others who come close to the female (doe or jill) he is guarding. Boxing, while they stand on their hind legs, usually takes place between a doe and a buck whose advances are premature.

HEDGES

'*If we never win a Test match again, we shall still have the world's finest hedges!*', Edmund Blunden exclaimed in 1935. '*Their white and red may, their bramble-roses, their wild-apple bloom, their honeysuckles, their traveller's joy, have been the spring of the year to most of us more inseparably than any other aspect of the season.'*

Sad to say, since 1950, more than half of our hedgerows have been ripped up – condemned as old-fashioned relics that shaded crops, sheltered vermin, wasted space and got in the way of farm machinery. For years the government paid farmers to bulldoze them out of existence. At last, in the 1990s, agri-environment schemes began to encourage care for those that remained and the planting of new ones. In 1997 the Hedge-rows Regulations made it illegal to remove most countryside hedgerows without planning permission. But hedges continue to be lost through neglect and bad management.

Those that survive are utterly various, legacies of diverse soil and climate and agricultural histories. A few are remnants of lost woods: at Shelley in Suffolk one unusual roadside hedge of woodland trees – small-leaved lime and service – is all that remains of the eighteenth-century Withers Wood. Most are planted; nowhere else has plotted and pieced its land in the same way. *'Hedges are good for intimacy, an enhanced sense of locality,'* Adam Nicolson wrote. *'That closeness of hedge-texture, the way in which they reflect and embody the nature of the particular place, is why they have such a hold on the English imagination.'*

The starkest contrast is between the 'champion' fields of the clay vales of the Midlands and the 'bosky', long-enclosed countryside of the South West. In the Midlands, where fields are large and regular in shape, hedges are typically thin, quickset (hawthorn), straight with right-angled corners, *'all very tidy – and dull',* opined the great landscape historian W.G. Hoskins. *'It is an artificial and comparatively modern landscape, and that is what is wrong with it, what makes it so unsatisfying, so unappealing to anybody born in the far west, beyond the Somerset plain.'*

The Midlands hedges were planned and planted only two hundred years ago, as common fields were parcelled out to landholders and enclosed. By contrast, in the ancient landscape of the South West, small, irregular fields are *'shut in by massive hedge-banks which are often faced with*

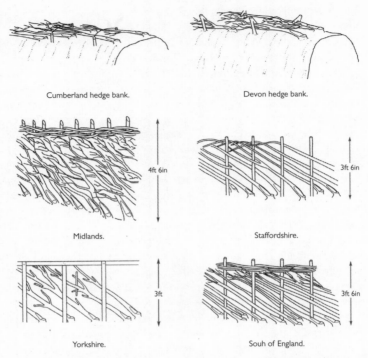

Cumberland hedge bank.

Devon hedge bank.

Midlands. 4ft 6in

Staffordshire. 3ft 6in

Yorkshire. 3ft

Souh of England. 3ft 6in

great blocks of native stone; and on top of these hedge-banks tall trees – sycamore, oak, ash and elm – grow freely,' Hoskins wrote. *'The hedge-banks are high and massive because they had to keep wild animals away from the stock – or give shelter to stock and crops – especially in Cornwall and west Devon where the salt Atlantic winds stunt even the trees.'* On Cornwall's Land's End peninsula, hedge banks that carry hardly any shrubs have been dated to the Bronze Age, ranking them among the world's oldest artefacts still in use.

Hedges still mark ancient boundaries, between manors, parishes or larger estates, in many parts of the country. Saxon settlers called the

Hedge-laying techniques.

hedge *haga*, derived from their name for the hawthorn fruit. In some places the hedge gave its name to the land it enclosed: Haigh in south Yorkshire and Manchester; Hagley in Herefordshire; Northaw in Hertfordshire; Thornhaugh in Northamptonshire.

If hedges imposed order and ownership on an evolving landscape, they also provided a valuable resource, especially as woodland declined during the medieval period. Hedge trees – oak, ash and elm – were often pollarded to produce a crop of fuel wood every decade or so. This practice also lengthened a tree's life; many ancient trees were once pollards in hedges. Hornbeam is popular in the South East, its hard wood valued for flails and mill machinery. On Exmoor beech standards tower above the beech hedges planted when the moor was enclosed in the nineteenth century.

Hedges provided fodder for livestock. Elm was a favourite 'leafy hay' in the Midlands, and many hedges composed entirely of elm are found on the south Essex plain and on the Dengie peninsula, as well as in parts of Kent, Suffolk and Worcestershire. Holly-rich hedges are plentiful in and around the Pennines and in parts of the South East – holly is stock-proof, tolerant of grazing, provides excellent winter forage for sheep and can thrive on poor, sandy soils. Kent still has a few tall hedges, once up to twenty feet tall, designed to shelter fields full of hops; alder is the preferred tall hedge for sheltering commercial orchards. Alder and willow are used in wet river valleys in Sussex, while buckthorn does well on chalky soils in Essex and Hertfordshire.

Crab, hazel, field maple, buckthorn, elder, dogwood, guelder rose, privet, wayfaring tree, sallow, bramble and a variety of roses – dog, burnet, field, sweet briar – all find their way into hedges. After hawthorn, the sloe, or blackthorn, is the most popular woody hedging plant. Like elm it is a suckering species, creating wide, dense hedges.

Lilac is a familiar feature of hedges on the sand soils of coastal Suffolk, while in parts of the South West fuchsias hedge small fields. On windswept Cornish coasts salt-tolerant tamarisk comes into its own. Hedges of gorse dot the New Forest. 'Deal rows' – lines of Scots pine – still grow in Breckland and on the Suffolk Sandlings in East Anglia; on the Elveden estate in Breckland these trees are still maintained as true hedges.

Fruit trees feature in old hedgerows, too. There are cherries in Norfolk, cider apples in Herefordshire, damsons in the Lyth valley, Westmorland and in Shropshire, too, with gooseberries and spindle near the villages of Shelve, Pennerley and Stiperstones, where squatters enclosed wasteland with hedges rich in fruit. Bullace, a wild plum, often partners crab apple in fruit hedges in Kent, Cheshire and Staffordshire, where it also supplied a dye for carpets or leather.

Hedgerows now form one of the last refuges for woodland and grassland species banished by development and intensive agriculture. Six hundred species of plant, 65 species of bird and twenty species of mammal have been recorded living in hedges. Some forty types of butterfly – two-thirds of the British list – depend on hedgerows, including the brimstone, green-veined white, comma, small tortoiseshell, peacock and hedge brown, or gatekeeper. Orange-tipped butterflies feed on cuckoo flowers at the roots, while the rare brown hairstreak spends its days in the tops of hedges. The hawthorn shield bug, dozens of bees and hoverflies and many of Britain's forty species of ladybird depend upon them – all in all, fifteen hundred species of insect rely on hedgerows, making them in turn a bonanza for insectivorous birds and bats.

In autumn and winter great flocks of fieldfares and redwings descend to raid the berries; bullfinches, blackbirds and mistle thrushes also exploit these natural harvests for vital cold-weather food. Many species find shelter and nesting places, including tree sparrows, dunnocks or hedge sparrows, wrens, robins, blackbirds, whitethroats, linnets, yellow-hammers and turtle doves.

Grey partridge, rabbits, wood mice, field voles, bank voles and common and pygmy shrews make homes among the roots, attracting sparrow-hawks, barn owls, little owls, kestrels and stoats to hunt along the hedge lines. Adders and grass snakes favour dry, sunny hedge banks, where badgers may sometimes dig setts, their spoil heaps soon colonised by elder. Hazel hedges can harbour the enigmatic dormouse. Hedges link hospitable enclaves across bleak agricultural landscapes.

Hedges are kept dense and stock-proof by plashing, or laying, in winter every few years. Techniques vary – more than a dozen local styles have evolved, reflecting the varied nature and role of hedges. The key is to cut the stems of the main shrubs three-quarters of the way through, bend them downwards and overlap. Come spring the bent stems sprout a thick fence of vertical growth. In the Midlands style of plashing, the hedge is severely cut back; the remaining shoots and branches, known as pleachers, are bent and woven around stakes of ash or hazel (stabbers) spaced at intervals. The bushy, or 'brush', side of each shrub faces the field, to protect new growth from browsing livestock; a ditch protects the other side. The result is a strong, thick hedge that should be able to withstand the weight of a bullock leaning against it.

In Bedfordshire it was common practice to lay each side in turn, with a few years' gap, to make sure that the hedge remained stock-proof. In Leicestershire hedge-laying produced very tall, thick growth – called bullfinches – to keep beef cattle in. By contrast the hedges of the South West tend to be laid lower and more densely, because they enclose sheep, which are better at getting through small gaps. In the South the often ditchless hedge is 'double-brushed', with spiky brushwood protruding on either side to render it stock-proof. A new style of laying, called Motor-way, has been devised: pleachers are laid in the direction of traffic flow to minimise damage from vehicles crashing through the hedge.

Cutting tools, such as the slasher and billhook, once displayed regional diversity, too; their use required great skill and the whole process was labour intensive. Today, most agricultural hedges are flailed with mechanical hedge cutters, adding to their degradation and often denying wild creatures a winter food source.

In Edmund Blunden's day the hedger and ditcher had already become rarer, but the hedge *'will last some time yet'*, he predicted in 1935. *'And when there are no more English hedges, and the expedient of barbed wire has carried the day everywhere, "Then shall the realm of Albion/Be brought to great confusion".*

HILLS

The enormous number of English place-names that refer to hills, high places, summits and mounds – whether in native Briton, Latin, Saxon, Welsh or Norse – demonstrates the importance of hills as sacred places, landmarks, beacons, places to meet (moots, like Mutlow, near Cambridge) or places to settle. British and Welsh words for hills and heights gave us Brent, Cannock, Creech, Pennard, Vobster, Malvern, Lydeard and Bredon. The Anglo-Saxons brought the *dun* of Swindon, Abingdon and Ashdown and added their own words to pre-extant ones to get bilingual hybrids. The name Pennard Hill in Somerset means Hillhill Hill: *pen* is Welsh; *ard* is a form of Gaelic.

Cumberland and Westmorland stand tall, overtopping hills with mountains, pikes, crags and fells. Millstone grit forms jagged edges in the Pennines, where tors stand out as natural sculptures with names such as 'Dancing Bear' and 'Hen Cloud'. Northumberland shares the Cheviots but faces off the Scots with the great resilient rocks of the Whin Sill, underpinning Hadrian's Wall and staring north.

Margaret Gelling, who has studied place-names and landscape, says that '*the Old English topographical vocabulary is at its most discriminating in the classification of hills and ridges, and this aspect of study can afford great pleasure to the informed observer. Here, most of all, we are seeing what the Anglo-Saxon settlers saw.*'

There are knolls and knowes, tumps and cops, ridges, edges and banks. Some hills have astonishing names – Thorpe Cloud, Roseberry Topping, Clougha Pike, Brown Clee, Hard Knott, The Yelds. Above Bovey Tracey in Devon, and Ilkley and Pickering in Yorkshire, there are moors. From Littlehampton, Sussex, you go up into the Downs, and from Market

Rasen, Lincolnshire, the Wolds. The Howgills, between the Lakes and the Yorkshire Dales, are fells, but the Cheviots, Chilterns, Clent, Quantocks and Malverns are hills.

Many hills are topped by burial places, prehistoric barrows or the hill-side cemeteries of the nineteenth century. The striking combination of abrupt hill with church on top suggests a place of some pre-Christian significance. These churches are generally dedicated to St Michael, as at Brent Tor in Devon, Breedon on the Hill in Leicestershire, Glastonbury and Burrator in Somerset. Our taming of these high places extended to their use as triangulation points for the Ordnance Survey; the concrete 'trig points' mark the tops of many inter-visible hills.

Hills have proved useful as places of defence, and hill-forts and castles have accentuated their impregnability – Nottingham Castle fortified a great bluff overlooking the Trent. Some we have refashioned; Tegg's Nose at Rainow, Cheshire is one of many bearing the scars of quarrying – hills have long been plundered for building stone, minerals and fuel.

Chosen for their conspicuousness, hills can be good places to rally a community, for warning beacons and as lookouts. Tout or toot hills

Malvern Hills, Worcestershire.

were places where people kept watch. Hambury Tout and Worbarrow Tout are high points on Dorset's coastal cliffs. At Tout on the Isle of Portland people watched out for the landing of smuggled goods.

St Catherine's Hill just outside Winchester, Hampshire overlooked a prodigious twentieth-century struggle, its quiet and poise lost to the building of the M3 straight through Twyford Down. On St George's Hill in Surrey people gather still to remember the Diggers, who for nearly half a year in 1649 staunchly attempted to change the world. Gerrard Winstanley said: *'if thou dost not act, thou dost nothing … I took my spade and went and broke ground upon George-hill in Surrey, thereby declaring freedome to the Creation, and that the earth must be set free from entanglements of Lords and Landlords, and that it shall become a common Treasury for all.'* They were violently evicted, though demonstrating against poverty and hunger, and continue to inspire.

Scutchamer Knob near the Hendreds in Oxfordshire speaks of the festivities and fairs of cloth workers (a 'scutcher' was used to beat out soaked and softened flax). Today a kite gathering enlivens the ridge beside Barbury Castle near Swindon once a month. Adventurous people parascend, paraglide and hang-glide across the country from White Sheet Hill in Wiltshire or Ingleborough in the Yorkshire Dales. Heading uphill, motor and bike enthusiasts seek out sections for racing, although on made roads these are mostly on private property, such as the Gurston Down Hillclimb in Wiltshire and Harewood Speed Hillclimb in Yorkshire.

Edward Elgar lived in Worcestershire and eulogised the Malverns, which stand up so strikingly above the Vale of the Severn. One hundred and fifty years earlier, Celia Fiennes, traveller and diarist, had called this *'the English Alps'*. Ralph Vaughan Williams titled one of his pieces of music *Wenlock Edge*, although it was at Leith Hill, Surrey and not in Shropshire where he started a music festival. Perhaps one of the most evocative of lines in English poetry is from *A Shropshire Lad*, in which A.E. Housman asks: *'What are those blue remembered hills …?'*

ICE SKATING IN THE OPEN AIR

John Evelyn and Samuel Pepys often noted in their diaries that the Thames was frozen over. On 9 January 1684 the weather was treacherously cold. John Evelyn *'went across the Thames on the ice, now become so thick as to bear not only streets of booths, in which they roasted meat, and had divers shops of wares, quite across as in a town, but coaches, carts and horses passed over'*.

On 24 January: *'Coaches plied from Westminster to the Temple, and from several other stairs to and fro, as in the streets, sleds, sliding with skates, a bull-baiting, horse and coach-races ... so that it seemed to be a bacchanalian triumph, or carnival on the water.'* These frost fairs took place *'once or twice every century until 1831'*, when *'the removal of Old London Bridge allowed the river above it to flow too fast to freeze solid'*, and the 'Little Ice Age' of the sixteenth to eighteenth centuries, which had gripped Europe and given Brueghel much inspiration, had slipped away.

Skating on the lakes and tarns of the Lake District, such as Rydal Water, Ratherheath Tarn, Tarn Hows, Derwent Water and Windermere, used to happen much more frequently than it does today. In his 'Country Diary' columns for the *Guardian*, A. Harry Griffin described how in the cold winter of 1929 the railways ran excursions from London and other cities to the 'Lakeland ice carnival', where *'there seemed as many people on and around the "toe" of Windermere as on a busy summer's day in Blackpool. And not only crowds of people on the ice but many cars parked on it, and roaring hot braziers as well.'* He recalled how he *'left the Lakeside crowds and skated northwards, completely alone, up the lake for two or three miles, with so far as I could see, the whole black ice of Windermere to myself. A happy memory of carefree winters that perhaps won't be repeated in these days of global warming.'*

The usually sleepy town of Sturminster Newton on the river Stour in Dorset has been transformed by the freezing of the river. In 1891, according to Rodney Legg, *'skating was indulged in by the light of Chinese and other* lanterns, and many of the persons were attired in fancy costume. The band played selections of music, and the scene was a most lively one.'

The ornamental lake in front of Nottingham University is rigged with lights and opens to skaters when the weather gives a hand. Following New York, London offers a small circle of ice among the office towers of Broadgate and the courtyard of Somerset House, both of which throng day and night with delighted learners and cool customers. But nothing can beat the excitement of wild skating. Since the 1950s land drainage schemes have meant that many of the safe places for skating – flood meadows – are no longer available.

INNS

'There is nothing which has yet been contrived by man by which so much happiness is produced as by a good tavern or inn,' Dr Johnson once eulogised. In the 1940s Thomas Burke could still write about the institution being 'as familiar in the national consciousness as the oak and the ash and the village green and the church spire'.

The decline of the inn in its traditional sense – as a place where a weary traveller could obtain food, drink and accommodation – has been swift. Railway hotels stole trade, and then cars contracted the distance between places and lessened the need for overnight stops. Holidaymakers wanted more, so inns evolved into hotels, such as the White Hart in Lewes, Sussex and the Lygon Arms in Broadway, Worcestershire. Other drivers just wanted a pub lunch, an evening meal or a quiet pint. Such was the change in aspect of the old coaching inns that John Black ruefully observed in 1974 that they often could be recognised by 'the forbidding "No Coaches" sign outside'.

The buildings that survive tell of former glories. Marlborough College, Wiltshire was once an inn. The Ship in Mere, Wiltshire and the George in Stamford, Lincolnshire still boast their arched entrances and large cobbled courtyards. The Talbot in Oundle, Northamptonshire has iron railings designed to protect the walls from carriage wheels. The New Inn in Gloucester and New Inn in Salisbury, Wiltshire date from as recently as the Middle Ages.

Many of the earliest inn users were pilgrims, plying the roads to Canterbury and Dover in Kent and Winchester in Hampshire. There is a Pilgrim's Rest in Battle, Sussex, and the Maison Dieu hostel in Dover is now the town hall. Geoffrey Chaucer's famous Canterbury pilgrims set off from the Tabard at Southwark, London, which was demolished in 1874. In 2003 its passing was marked by the unveiling of a blue plaque in Chaucer's honour.

Beyond Chaucer, literature is frequently enriched by colourful inns: *Tom Jones*, *Lavengro*, *Silas Marner*, *Middlemarch*, the works of Dickens and G.K. Chesterton's *The Flying Inn*. The reality of the inn could be livelier than the fiction, with characters as unsavoury as the Jarmans of the Crane (now the Ostrich) in Colnbrook, Buckinghamshire, who murdered their guests in a vat of boiling ale.

Where not built for the church, inns may have been related to the lords of the manor, such as the Gloucester Arms in Penrith, Cumberland. Others were for the benefit of workers: labourers on the New Bedford River (the Hundred Foot Drain) in Cambridgeshire stayed in The Anchor at Sutton Gault. In nearby Lincolnshire the Leagate Inn

at Coningsby was a 'guide house', where safe passage across the Fens was arranged. Inns called the Ferry, their foundations on dry land, served as a pausing point for those in wait for a river or estuary crossing.

Inns were always closely linked to roads. The toll cottage opposite the Spaniards Inn in Hampstead, northwest London is a fair indicator of the

The White Swan, Pickering, Yorkshire.

symbiotic relationship between the two. Further north, inns were essential to the packhorse and coaching routes across desolate and often snow-filled passes. The Tan Hill Inn in Yorkshire is the highest, but the Kirkstone Pass Inn in Cumberland is equally remote, waiting at the top of a road known bleakly as The Struggle. The stagecoach was defeated by this road, passengers having to get out and walk to the inn along the most troublesome section. Ye Horns Inn in Goosnargh, Lancashire was a popular stopping-off point for packhorse trains.

Places where people from far and near could meet one another, it is not surprising that inns always had an important place in the community, whether for gossip or trade. Many inns carry particularity in their styles and building materials, and some became known for their food: the landlord of the Bell Inn at Stilton, Huntingdonshire offered cheese to travellers on the London coach.

JACK AND JILL

The hill referred to in the Jack and Jill rhyme is in Kilmersdon, a village midway between Bath and Wells in Somerset. The story goes that in the reign of Henry VIII, Jack and Jill, a married couple, were collecting their daily pail of water from the well (strangely up the hill) when a boulder from the quarry at Bad Stone, later known as Batson, rolled down and killed Jack. Jill, who was pregnant, died soon after giving birth to her son. The surname Gilson means Jill's son and, according to the village's website, '*there are more Gilsons in the area than in the whole of Manchester, Birmingham and Liverpool combined*'.

Kilmersdon, Somerset.

Visitors to the village may not know its connections with the nursery rhyme, but a discreet sign recently carved in low relief on a wall directs one to the hill. This is an example of small-scale public art at its best. 'Milestones', with fragments of the rhyme carved into them, lead the way along the path up the hill, renamed Jack and Jill Hill, to the restored well, which sits by the primary school at the top. The rhyme is cut into big slabs of slate attached to the school wall, and Jack and Jill with their pail are depicted on the metal entrance gates.

Little Jack Horner, who was caught with his thumb in a pie, lived not far away in Mells. He was steward to the last abbot of Glastonbury. His real name was Tom, but 'Jack' might refer to his knavishness in allegedly stealing the deeds to the Manor of Mells, which were hidden in a pie together with the deeds to eleven other manors – a gift from the ill-fated abbot to the King at the Dissolution. Tom Horner's descendants, who are convinced we have the wrong man, still live in Mells.

It is difficult to find reason in some of our nursery rhymes. 'Humpty Dumpty' seems particularly hard to crack. Some argue that the rhyme refers to a cannon positioned on the city walls close to St Mary's-at-the-Wall Church in Colchester, Essex, which was used by the Royalists in the Civil War to defend the city during the siege of 1648. According to Jean Harrowven, Humpty Dumpty was a wooden war machine, used by Charles I to gain the City of Gloucester from the Roundheads. While being rolled downhill and across the river, it was irre-trievably broken – *all the king's horses and all the king's men* could do nothing.

Banbury Museum coyly notes that *By today's standards the words of many early rhymes seem strikingly unsuitable for those of tender years*, in a leaflet that struggles not to mention the possible sexual con-notations in this Oxfordshire rhyme:

Banbury, Oxfordshire.

Ride a cock-horse to Banbury Cross,
To see a fine lady upon a white horse;
Rings on her fingers and bells on her toes,
And she shall have music wherever she goes.

This is an old verse, but it was first published in 1744 and more widely between 1784 and 1877 in chap-books for children; over the years the words have changed. There were three crosses in Banbury in the Middle Ages – White Cross, Bread Cross and High or Market Cross – all of which were destroyed by the Puritans in about 1600. The cross that stands now at Horse Fair, built in 1859, is not the cross in the rhyme.

There is much dispute as to the identity of the 'fine lady'. Celia Fiennes, who travelled the country on horseback in 1697, is one suggestion; Lady Godiva, another. Others believe she was an earth goddess and part of a pagan spring ritual. A cock-horse means a *'high-spirited horse'*, according to *The Oxford Dictionary of Nursery Rhymes*, a child's hobby-horse and the name given to an additional horse harnessed to pull coaches up steep hills.

Banbury is now riding on the rhyme. In June 2000 an annual celebration of hobby-horse and animal-disguise customs was initiated and has started to draw jovial beasts from across the country.

KERBSTONES

Two familiar stories come from different ends of the country but echo the same cry for perpetuation of detail and quality in situ. Residents of Wallsend, Northumberland wrote to a local newspaper in 2003: *'We are writing to express our disgust at the removal of the original kerbstones from our back lanes and the manner in which it was done. No consultation. No explanation. Ugly tarmac casually slapped down in their place and the fact that the stones are to go to another "more deserving area". There is pride in the small things of quality in Wallsend, but soon there'll be nothing to be proud of, if our council continues to act in this disgraceful manner.'*

In Bradford-on-Avon, Wiltshire a town councillor told us in 2001 that he had *'found a stone wall demolished and a very wide new pavement being installed. Noticing concrete kerbstones being installed with original stone kerbstones discarded, I asked if they could be rescued.'*

Once an area is designated as deserving of conservation, the remainder is not lavished with such care. Simple things, such as kerbstones and flags, long a part of a neighbourhood, are often traded down to off-the-peg concrete then lost, sold privately or removed to a conservation area.

Poole in Dorset is notable in parts of its coniferous suburbs for grass running into the road; in many rural settlements this is also valued. In Bonsall, Derbyshire, according to the village design statement, *'The absence of pavements and kerbstones is characteristic of the village.'* In Great Bowden, Leicestershire the village design statement observes that *'Around the Green and on some other streets the road kerbs are still the attractive granite, which assists in retaining the link with bygone times. Along Sutton and Knights End Roads the verges are without kerbs; to maintain their rural character they need to be kept that way.'*

Civic societies strive to remind municipal authorities to value the particularity of a village or town's old kerbstones and prevent the unnecessary imposition of kerbs that suburbanise the countryside.

Most early roads and streets were mud, at best simply strewn with gravel and sand from the local gravel pit; a differentiated paved footway rarely existed. Road surfaces in the city might be of rough stones or cobbles with a kennel or drain running down the middle, and possibly a stone flag pavement on either side.

The development of new estates, such as Bedford and Belgravia in London, led to a raising of standards. The Westminster Paving Act of 1762 gave responsibility for the condition of roads to Paving Commissioners, who could 'impose a rate' to fund street improvements. It demanded stone kerbs, replacement of central drains with kerbside gutters and raising the pavement above the road surface to make walking a safer and drier experience. A precedent was set for other London estates, towns and cities, and many towns were paved in the late 1700s.

Coastal quarries began to do well – Purbeck stone was even specified to replace pebbles in some London streets by the 1762 Act. Granite was sought, being durable, impervious to water and aesthetically pleasing. Trade developed around the coast, much came from Aberdeen quarries to London, and coastal towns without their own hard rock found themselves kerbed with granite from Cornwall, Dartmoor, Lundy and the Lake District. As the canals extended and the railways came, rock from Charnwood Forest began to travel out of Leicestershire.

In Kentish Town, north London the kerbstones are edged with pink granite, white granite and diorite, filled with dark enclosures known by quarrymen as heathens and to geologists as xenoliths and enclaves. Geologist Eric Robinson describes a small section of the Mile End Road in east London: '*the thin kerbstones offer us blue and veined Channel Island diorites, speckled Cornish Granite, dull red Mountsorrel Granite, and a few dark grey Aberdeenshire Granite lengths*'.

In many places distinctiveness is a result of quality rather than local-ness, although in Loughborough, Leicestershire '*the old pink kerbstones made of local granite from Mountsorrel show the chisel marks of the quarrying instruments*', according to a local website. In Derbyshire, Barry Joyce pointed out that '*The old causeys (pavements) are under threat … each area had its own tradition of paving, based on locally available materials.*' In The Dale in Wirksworth limestone paving is still edged by limestone kerbs from Dale Quarry up the road. There are examples in Norfolk of the use of brick where the local material is not hard enough. In Bridgnorth, Shropshire the pavements are of hard yellow engineering bricks with the gutters in big blue tiles.

LANDMARK TREES

Many trees have been endowed with significance. The Meavy Oak, eight hundred years old, was where the people of this Dartmoor village gathered; the Tolpuddle Martyrs' sycamore in Dorset was the focus of an early agricultural workers' protest. Gospel oaks mark places of preaching on the parish boundary at Rogationtide; the Boscobel Oak in Shropshire is remembered for concealing Charles II.

On tithe maps and old estate maps, boundary trees are often marked individually: crab-apple and oak, for example, being long-lived, were appropriate for this purpose. Richard Mabey noted that '*The highly distinctive appearance of black poplars meant they were also employed as landmark trees. One ancient, weatherbeaten tree (c. 200 years old), in the Bourne Gutter near Berkhamsted (Hertfordshire), marks the intersection of parish, manor and county boundaries.*'

Trees were used not only to demarcate territory, but as visual signposts, different species or groupings having distinct meanings. Katrina Porteous says that '*Trees have always been important to north Northumberland fishermen. Individual trees or groups of trees (known as "plantin's") serve as landmarks for navigation (less important now due to the increased use of electronic navigational instruments). Some examples seen from Beadnell include Heiferlaw, Shepherd's Cottage Plantin', Beadnell Trees.*'

In the nineteenth century trees were often used as road signs. According to J.H. Wilks, an ash and sycamore were planted together at strategic points to warn of dangerous places. '*The combination became known as John and Mary, and was recognised as an old form of warning of crossroads or of a main road ahead.*' In north Devon two

Beeches, near Beaford, Devon.

beech trees planted on either side of a farm lane are known as 'mother and father' trees. Male and female black poplars were planted close to one another for propagation, as were monkey-puzzles by the Victorians.

Yews line drove roads through Hampshire and are planted along a drove in Ashdown Forest, Sussex. Three yews signified accommodation for animals and people; two meant people only. A few Scots pines frequently advertised places where drovers/travellers could stay. Trees marking the start of turnpike roads were later replaced by toll-houses. At Boddington in Gloucestershire a hollow tree with a wainscoted interior, 54 feet in circumference at its base in the 1780s, is thought to have been used as a room for taking tolls.

'Mile trees' are depicted on early maps. A seventeenth-century map shows eight mile trees on the Racecourse Way in Wiltshire. William Stukeley described them further in 1723: along *the road from Wilton to Shaftesbury, called the "Ten Mile Course" … a traveller is indebted to Lord Pembroke for reviving the Roman method of placing a numbered stone at every mile, and the living index of a tree to make it more observable*'. The trees were limes, planted at around the same time as the milestones in 1700. A correspondent to *The Times* in November 1960 traced several of them, but none seems to have survived.

It would be refreshing to see more imaginative and meaningful tree planting in England. In 1993 Common Ground proposed a scheme called County Entrances, to encourage the planting of locally typical trees on roads at county boundaries, but at the time boundaries were under review – another good reason to mark the traditional counties that have stood the test of time.

LETTERBOXING

Rather like entrusting a letter to a bottle at sea, in 1854 a Dartmoor guide called James Perrott put his visiting card in a glass jar. He placed it in a bank at a remote place called Cranmere Pool near the source of the West Okement river, presumably hoping that someone would find it.

Intrepid walkers who came across Perrott's card added their own and, by 1888, the jar had been replaced by a tin box that could accommodate more. In 1905 two walkers put a visitors' book in the box, which attracted 1,741 signatures in three years. People began to enclose self-addressed and stamped postcards to be sent on by the next visitor from his home town.

Similar boxes appeared on Belstone Tor in 1894 and at Duck's Pool on South Moor in 1938, to commemorate the Dartmoor writer William Crossing. In 1976 fifteen letterboxes were included in a guide and their numbers proliferated. The Dartmoor National Park Authority proposed to ban the practice, since ancient cairns were being desecrated, but a campaign to save them, led by the *Western Morning News*, resulted in an agreed code of conduct.

The letterboxes at Duck's Pool and Cranmere Pool are made of stone and appear on Ordnance Survey maps. Most of the others – there are over 3,000 registered boxes and many more unrecorded ones – are secreted under stones, in hollows and caves, often discovered only with the help of cryptic clues or by word of mouth.

Letterbox hosts (anyone can place and register a box, as long as they maintain it) are beginning to make rubber stamps bearing emblems – a running fox for Fox Tor, an adder for Willtor Clitter, an engine house for Hooten Wheals – so that visitors can stamp their own books. A new folk art has arisen. New versions of the stamps may be put into boxes each year or for special occasions, and some boxes contain rewards (such as miniature bottles of whisky) for the first person who finds the new issue. Letterboxes not only celebrate the wildlife and natural features of the moor, but also its industrial past, including peat digging, tin mining, glass making, quarrying and charcoal burning. Instead of signing the visitors' book, regular letterboxers, such as the Moorons and the Brixham Grasshoppers, use their own personal stamps.

In the early 1980s Godfrey Swinscow started the Dartmoor Letterboxes 100 Club for people who have visited more than a hundred boxes; it now has at least twelve thousand members. It publishes a catalogue of Dartmoor Letterboxes, with clues to their locations, twice a year.

MANHOLE COVERS

Beneath your feet on most urban streets is a fascinating array of iron grate and manhole cover designs: grids of raised squares; parallelograms arranged in floral patterns; spokes radiating out from a central hub; chequers. Manhole covers have prompted everything from rubbings to an exhibition in 2001 called 'Quilts from Manhole Covers'.

Cast-iron covers, big enough for a man to climb through, appeared in the late eighteenth century for access down to some of the necessary aspects of urban life. The majority are round to stop them falling down the holes. Rectangular ones tend to indicate a shallower drain or hole.

Manhole covers.

The newly industrialised towns, with their foundries, beat out the iron discs and oblongs, their places of origin given pride of place in raised letters. Nineteenth-century Derbyshire had iron ore and foundries in almost all of its towns: Chartres and Son made covers for the Melbourne Sanitary Board; Stanton originally for Stanton by Dale. Now Stanton Warriors are found everywhere. On a perambulation around Consett in Durham, Katrina Porteous found the works of manufacturers from Durham, Sunderland, Bishop Auckland and Newcastle.

One Devon engineer pointed out that the roadside grates, once made locally for local conditions, are now the same across the county (and the country), and they do not do nearly as good a job in clearing water.

Smaller covers have a role. In nineteenth-century London Haywards of Union Street made the coal plates that punctuate pavements around Hampstead and Bloomsbury. They enabled coal to be directly shot into cellars beneath the pavement.

In the twenty-first century London is pioneering new cover design. As part of the regeneration of Deptford in the south east, a number of artists have been invited to contribute street furniture: Geoff Rigden is providing manhole covers made of bronze.

MOON

It is full moon in March and people along the tidal Trent await the aegir. At full moons between Easter and Lammas, off Colchester and Whitstable, the oysters are spatting (not fighting, but spawning). Our calendar, once driven by the sun and moon, still keeps the moveable feast of Easter on *'the first Sunday after the full moon which happens on or next following the 21st of March the Spring Equinox: and if the full moon happens upon a Sunday, Easter-day is the Sunday following'* (Book of Common Prayer); upon this date rest many others in the Christian panoply of festivals.

Coal-hole cover.

Sun day and Moon day are still part of our daily lives. Chinese New Year begins on the eve of the new moon on the last day of the twelfth lunar month, and ends fifteen days later with the full moon some time in January or February. Psalm 81 calls up the Jewish new year, Rosh Hashanah, in September: '*Sound the horn on the new moon.*' This is the annual celebration of the creation of the

world, the day of judgment and the reinforcement of Israel's bond with God. The Hindu, Sikh and Jain new year is celebrated on the night of the new moon in the month of Karttika in October to November.

A glimpse of the full moon between the verticals of the city offers a rare reminder of one's link with the cosmos. People who live and work by the sea are attuned to the ebb and flow of the moon through the tides; at new and full moon come the higher spring tides, and at the mid-points of waxing and waning come the neap, or lower, tides.

Working or walking under the harvest moon in late September, one is struck by its brilliance, by the starkness of shadows and the brightness of badgers. Moonless and cloudless nights give us the full glory of the Milky Way, if we are lucky enough to live under pollution-free, dark skies.

As it becomes ever harder to find a really dark place to ponder the stars and the moon, fields with moon names offer their own attractions. The meanings of Moonshiney, Moon Mead, Moon Piece and Moon Field remain obscure, although some may be describing the shape, as in Half Moon. Moon Hill in Sussex perhaps describes a natural topographical crescent on the flank of the hill. It is possible that other things may be implied, as John Field pointed out in relation to Moonfield in Great and Little Munden in Hertfordshire: '*It may allude to a location favoured for moonlight activities, such as poaching.*'

Moonless nights were preferred for moving brandy. The Man in the Moon appears on many pub signs; he is at the heart of folktales, which

Medieval stained-glass window, St Andrew's Church, Mells, Somerset.

have him as a light-fingered peasant making off with brushwood over his shoulder, as Shakespeare described in *A Midsummer Night's Dream*:

> *One must come in with a bush of thorns and a lantern,*
> *And say he comes to disfigure, or to present,*
> *The person of Moonshine.*

Moon daisy is an older name than ox-eye, and still goes by the name of moon flower or moon's eye in Somerset, moon penny in Cheshire and, simply, moons in Berkshire, Buckinghamshire, Cambridgeshire, Cheshire, Essex, Gloucestershire, Warwickshire, Wiltshire, Worcestershire and Yorkshire. Geoffrey Grigson reminded us that its time is midsummer and its other names link it with thunder and the sun.

The people of Wiltshire are known as Moonrakers, from a tale that echoes that of the Mad or Wise Men of Gotham, Nottinghamshire, who went fishing for the moon. Alice Oswald takes up the tale:

> *... and they threw the net,*
> *They steered away, they pulled the running cord,*
> *The net turned over like a purse, it rose*
> *Into the moon and through the moon and out;*
> *The moon broke up in pieces and came whole.*
> *Three times they cast the driftnet, saw the net*
> *Grope for a ghost and gather what it could*
> *And ropes of water reeve themselves away.*

Rolling cheeses downhill to send them off to market on their own, drowning eels, building cuckoo pounds, trying to catch the reflection of the moon ... By all accounts the stories of the exploits of these loony villagers was sufficient to cause King John to give them a wide berth in his peregrinations, saving the village a great deal of effort and money.

NOMANSLAND

Nomansland appears as a settlement name in Wiltshire, Hertfordshire and Devon, and, as a more intimate place-name, describes land on the edge of a parish, often common land.

No Man's Heath lies at the junction of the counties of Derbyshire, Leicestershire, Staffordshire and Warwickshire. Between north Yorkshire and County Durham, above Arkengarthdale, one area was sufficiently contested to be called The Disputes. No Man's is a community orchard purchased in the 1990s by the neighbouring parishes of Chartham Hatch and Harbledown in Kent. Each year on Apple Day they hold a tug-of-war across the parish boundary, proving that a boundary need not be a frontier.

ORCHARDS

Old orchards are the richest kind. Some have occupied the same land for centuries. The orchard at Bawdrip in Somerset has been traced on maps back to at least 1575. Yet the land was contested for seven years, with repeated applications and appeals for houses, despite local opposition. The continuity of land use makes for rich wildlife, long-told stories and a deeper sense of loss.

Orchards and individual fruit trees are found in every county, but the major commercial fruit-growing areas remain Cambridgeshire, Devon, Essex, Herefordshire, Kent, Somerset and Worcestershire. Kent grows eating and cooking apples, cherries, pears, plums and cobnuts; the eastern counties apples; the South West cider apples, perry pears and mazzards (cherries); the Vale of Evesham apples, plums and pears. Cherries were grown extensively in Hertfordshire and Berkshire, damsons in Cumberland and Westmorland, apples in Middlesex.

Orchards, with their tall, 'standard' trees, are important in the landscape. Current commercial orchards are of dense lines of small trees; some are so intensive they are more like vineyards. By contrast, standard cider apples were spaced on a thirty-foot grid, and the majestic cherries on the north Kent coast more than forty feet from one another. Tall perry pears were planted every sixty feet. Under them sheep might graze; sometimes flowers or soft fruit would be grown.

Orchards are like wood pasture, full of micro-habitats, their biodiversity no less rich for having been sustained through nurture by many hands. They tell the seasons frankly, flaunting blossom, dropping fruit, enticing creatures large and small, enjoying winter wassailing. They display an intricacy of particularity to place. In Westmorland, damson trees keep company with stone walls, in Shropshire they march along hedgerows, as do cherries in some parts of Norfolk. Giant cherry trees, sixty feet high, gather in (the few remaining) orchards around Faversham, Kent, while further south in the Weald, squat cobnut plats pick out the ragstone of the Greensand ridge.

Newly planted elder trees are remaking the landscape in Leicester-shire and Surrey as the demand for elderflower cordial grows. Hereford, Somerset and Devon are renowned for their cider-apple orchards. Gloucestershire, despite losing three-quarters of its orchards since 1945, still has many kinds of perry pear. These huge, long-lived trees (they can reach 60 feet and 350 years) are so par-

ticular about their conditions that some varieties will not grow more than five miles from where they arose; each parish produced its own single-variety perry or local blend.

Every farm and big garden had its own orchard of mixed fruit trees for domestic use, and farm labourers were often part-paid in cider. In Ryedale, Yorkshire

George Morris discovered that on marriage a woman would move to her husband's farm, taking with her graft wood to add to the orchard, which would be her domain. Typically in apples alone there would be Yorkshire Cockpit, Green Balsam, Yorkshire Greening (also called Yorkshire Goose Sauce), Backhouse Flowery Town (with its pink flesh), Yorkshire Beauty, Keswick Codling, Warner's King, Lane's Prince Albert, Dog's Snout, Catshead, Burr Knot, Striped Beefing, Gravenstein, Lemon Pippin and Northern Greening.

Apparently the latter are often grubbed out now as people do not realise that their hard and sour early persona is transformed by Easter. The whaling ships making their way from Whitby in Yorkshire to the southern ocean would carry apples that took perhaps six months to mature, ensuring a supply of vitamin C against scurvy (long before oranges). Orchards around the Vale of York finally crashed in numbers when Rowntree began to use chemical pectin to set its fruit gums.

When we lose an orchard we sacrifice not simply a few old trees (bad enough, some would say), but we risk losing forever varieties particular to the locality, together with wildlife, songs, recipes, cider, festive gatherings, the look of the landscape and the wisdom gathered over generations about pruning and grafting, aspect and slope, soil and season, variety and use. We sever our links with the land.

Looked at from a different angle, if we lose real cider we lose the need for cider barrels, flagons, wassail bowls, mugs, tools, troughs, presses ... people. We lose interest in artefacts and buildings often unique to their place. They are devalued, left to rot, mislaid, broken up, and with them fades the knowledge, the self-esteem and soon the varieties, the wildlife, and so on. Everything is dependent upon everything else; culture and nature, when so finely tuned, create a dynamic, intimately woven working world.

It would be wrong to assume that the city is bereft of orchards. Norwich, it was famously mused, 'was either a city in an orchard or an orchard in a city'. In north London, in 1989, the Hampstead Garden Suburb

Horticultural Society organised a great apple hunt to identify garden fruit trees planted by Dame Henrietta Barnett in 1899. More than forty varieties were rediscovered scattered across the front and back gardens, making an extensive orchard. Because fruit trees can be trained to take up little space, the idea of creating espaliers against walls in the smallest of city gaps is a feasible proposition, and there are now parks and allotments that await the fruits of newly planted small orchards.

Many old orchards are being lost to other forms of agriculture (since fruit is so cheap on the world market) and to building. Wiltshire has lost 95 per cent of its orchards since 1945, Devon ninety per cent since 1965. For many counties the loss is more than two-thirds. But much renewed interest in orchards has stemmed from recognising the links between variety and place. Community, city and school orchards are being created with varieties that are local to the parish, town and county, reinvigorating knowledge and keeping it practised in its locality.

PARKS

Until the nineteenth century recreation happened in the streets, in the fields, on the commons or at fairgrounds, such as Newcastle's Town Moor or Oxford's Port Meadow. The Victorians tended to see these as debased places, where immoral things went on, and began to establish more edifying public parks for healthy exercise. Man could be enlightened by Art, and Nature tamed. Highly manicured, parks were partly about teaching nature and people 'good manners'. Battersea Park in London was built to supersede the wilder Battersea Field. Derby Arboretum, with its grand entrance lodge (now a photographic gallery and workshop), and Birkenhead Park in Cheshire were among the earliest municipal parks. The latter's grandeur inspired New York's Central Park. Seaside and spa towns also took on the park ideal, with promenade gardens.

These Victorian parks were typified by neat landscaping and elaborate fixtures, such as bandstands, fountains, aviaries – particularly ornate are those at Darwen in Lancashire and Penzance's Morrab Subtropical Garden in Cornwall – sculptures and statues, including Peter Pan in Kensington Gardens and the dinosaurs at Crystal Palace Park, both in London.

Towards the end of the twentieth century parks were seen as a burden – difficult and expensive to maintain, abused by drug pushers, unsafe and unsavoury. People had fled. With the cost-cutting Local Government Act in 1988 local authorities had to find the cheapest ways of looking after their open spaces, by putting jobs such as grounds maintenance out to 'compulsory competitive tendering'. Out went apprenticeships, groundsmen, park keepers and real gardeners; in came roving contract staff with no attachment to place, plants imported rather than grown internally. Knowledge and pride were lost, parks deteriorated in quality.

But those that held their traditions have not declined and maintain a special place in the hearts of people, as a green escape in town, a quiet retreat at lunchtime, for jogging, relaxing with the children or feeding the ducks. More wildlife management means more wildflowers than municipal beds, more wild creatures than ornamental birds. Some are well-known venues for melas and free concerts, with a 'keep on the grass' attitude.

England's parks received more than 296 million visits each year at the end of the last century. New attitudes are emerging, councils are recognising that open space is not for car parking but vital to the quality of life of ordinary families and workers. Now millions of pounds are being spent to restore parks betrayed by the mean measures of the 1980s.

PROMENADES

Promenading under avenues of trees became popular in the seventeenth and eighteenth centuries; any town with pretensions to gentility had its parade, walk or promenade. The fashion for strolling, being seen, observing and taking tea began to extend to the seaside, with promenades describing polite society as well as the edge of the land.

The development of coastal resorts began at Scarborough, Yorkshire in 1700, where the first Spa House by the sea was built as it became fashionable to walk or promenade along the beach as well as taking the waters. Esplanades, or sea-side promenades, were built partly as sea defences, but the trend for social walking meant that they offered a wider attraction. The first was developed at Weymouth, Dorset in the 1770s, after the construction of the earliest resort building to face the sea.

Genteel Sidmouth in Devon has less than a mile of esplanade tucked between the red rocks of the bay; it was built in 1837 after the railway arrived, and featured a library, which sold books and roll-out panoramas of the sea front. On the Wirral in Cheshire New Brighton's wide Marine Promenade, built on sand-dunes by a speculator in the 1830s, offered a destination for Liverpool's day trippers on a ferry across the Mersey.

Blackpool, Lancashire.

I do like to stroll along the prom, prom, prom,
Where the brass bands play
Tiddly-om-pom-pom

Promenades are bordered by decorative iron-work railings, lamps, seats and Victorian shelters, intended for winter use as well as breezy summer days. The Golden Mile in Blackpool, Lancashire, with its wide, busy promenade and tramways, has ornate nineteenth-century wind shelters, piers, rides and the 518-foot-high Tower, which opened in 1894. As part of the rebuilding of the sea defences on the south shore, three new wind shelters, a striking and graceful design by Ian McChesney, rotate with the prevailing wind. The accepted health benefits of sea air and the sea resorts that established themselves during the last two centuries have left an enduring association with rest and recuperation as well as the bright lights and bustle of the resorts. Skegness is still '*so bracing!*', as the Great Northern Railway poster of 1923–47 proclaimed, and a walk on the prom proves it.

QUARTERS

Chichester, Sussex is divided by North, East, South and West thorough-fares, a physical memory of the Roman Empire. Latin quarters they are not, but increasingly we use 'quarter' to relate to neighbourhoods with recognisable identities, especially when 'regeneration' is in the air.

It has become *de rigueur* to contemplate the revival of parts of cities in terms of social or working 'quarters', usually based around old street patterns and buildings of character that cry out for new uses. In its *City Centre Strategy* of 1994, Sheffield identified eleven quarters. The Cathedral Quarter characteristically has steep lanes. Derelict warehouses taken on by Yorkshire ArtSpace, which created a draw that brought artists, musicians and film makers together in the 1980s, is dulled with the title of Cultural Industries Quarter. The street layout is based on that of the eighteenth century, when small businesses set up with impressive façades in front of workshops, frequently rented by the so-called Little Mesters, self-employed cutlery makers.

Artists are often at the heart of unplanned re-creation of belief in an area. Spike Island in Bristol and, in east London, Wapping, then Hackney, then Hoxton owe much to the willingness of artists to create communities in cheap and interesting, run-down parts of town. Their inevitable displacement by 'risk-taking' developers is the greatest irony.

Authenticity can be elusive, but spearheaded by Birmingham's Irish Community Forum, Digbeth has become the city's Irish Quarter, centred on the culverted river Rea, an area settled long ago by the navvies who built the canals and much of the Victorian city. Bradford's Victorian warehousing area, centred on the now demolished Exchange Station, was known as Little Germany because of the resident family businesses.

Birmingham has been busy restoring buildings in the Jewellery Quarter. Hull's Museums Quarter embraces four museums in the High Street, including Wilberforce House. These are a far cry from the vibrancy of London's cosmopolitan Soho or Pakistani, Sikh and Sri Lankan Southall, which speak of identity being generated spontaneously as opposed to being manufactured and marketed.

RIVERS

Seeing a man sitting quietly cross-legged with flowers and fruit spread out before him on the city banks of the river Tyne is to glimpse quiet communion with nature. Increasingly rivers in England are standing in for sacred rivers on other continents. For Hindus and Sikhs the Ganga is the most sacred of rivers, but to scatter the ashes of loved ones is difficult if you live and die in England. Water from the Ganga has been brought to the rivers Thames, Wye and Soar to bless them as places for ritual.

Between Barrow upon Soar and Mountsorrel in Leicestershire families gather to scatter flowers, powder, tulsi grass and holy leaves. Amid chanting and the ringing of bells, the ashes of the dead are committed to the river, which runs to the sea, transporting them to the next life.

Ancient votive offerings of swords and gold have been found in many of our rivers. Stories, legends and myths still cling. The spirit Peg o' Nell took one life in seven in the Yorkshire Ribble; the Dart in Devon was said to claim one life a year – '*Dart, Dart, cruel Dart/Every year thou claimst a heart*' – and the Trent, in Nottinghamshire and Lincolnshire, three. The Tweed is appeased by the casting of salt over water and nets. These stories are likely to be very old, and worth the retelling for that alone, but they also give us hints of who has settled here and their preoccupations, and what persistence the old gods still have.

A river catchment is united by the water within it – groundwater, springs, streams and rivers. If you tamper with one part it has repercussions on the rest. Because of demands on the groundwater in the Chilterns, the river Misbourne in Buckinghamshire is now dry along part of its length.

In the north of its catchment the Dorset Stour betrays the intricate branching typical of tributaries on clay, whereas, lower down, the simpler feeder streams speak of chalk. The patterns that rivers make tell their story. The steep and narrow yet winding course of the Wye tells us of rising land. Neither land nor sea stays still, and the river ruled by gravity never runs straight. Ruskin captured this: '*All rivers, small or large, agree in one character, they like to lean a little on one side: they cannot bear to have their channels deepest in the middle, but will always, if they can, have one bank to sun themselves upon, and another to get cool under.*' A river left to its own

Catchment of the river Stour, Wiltshire, Somerset, Dorset, Hampshire.

devices reinvents itself all the time, through meanders, pools, waterfalls, ox bows, backwaters, cliffs, islands and long linear edges that juxtapose two very different worlds, each of which enriches the other.

The interface between water and land offers a great range of the richest habitats of all: one-third of our indigenous plants, about six hundred species, according to English Nature, are found in or by rivers. The assemblages of fish vary in different parts of a river and between catchments. The vegetation fringing riverbanks is crucially important for wildlife, providing safe staging and living places for birds, water voles and otters.

But few rivers have been allowed to remain 'natural'. Straight, featureless drains are deserts. This recognised, farmers increasingly are encouraged to leave wide riparian buffer strips, which also minimise the risk of fertilisers and pollutants reaching watercourses. Field names that imply wetness are a good place to start restoration planning: Drunken Field (waterlogged land), Feggy Leasow (marshy land), Flaggy Doles (land on which marsh plants grow), Mizzey (muddy land), Plashets (marshy place), The Orles (land on which alders grow). Each river has a propensity towards difference.

> *Rivers arise; whether thou be the Son*
> *Of utmost Tweed, or Oose, or gulphie Dun,*
> *Or Trent, who like some earth-born Giant spreads*
> *His thirty Armes along the indented Meads,*
> *Or sullen Mole that runneth underneath,*
> *Or Severn swift, guilty of Maidens death,*
> *Or Rockie Avon, or of Sedgie Lee,*
> *Or Coaly Tine, or ancient hallowd Dee,*
> *Or Humber loud that keeps the Scythians Name,*
> *Or Medway smooth, or Royal Towred Thame.*

JOHN MILTON, from 'Rivers arise; whether thou be the Son'

ROCKS

On the wall of Stone Farm at Blaxhall, Suffolk is a sign: '*THE BLAXHALL STONE: Said to have been ploughed up in the 19th century when no bigger than two fists, thrown down by the ploughman where it now stands, it has been growing ever since.*' Stories surface here and there of fields growing stones and of stones themselves expanding or mothering pebbles.

Huge rocks naturally out of place have sometimes been deposited by ice. The War Stone sits on a plinth in Warstone Lane in central Birmingham; a glacial erratic, it was used as a hoar stone, or boundary marker, from which its name drifted, in the process naming a cemetery and a brewery. In the Forest of Bowland in Yorkshire and Lancashire many erratic boulders have been used for boundary markers; the most extraordinary is the Great Stone of Fourstones on Tatham Fells. Where the other three have gone hardly seems to matter, this one is so huge – it has a hewn staircase of fourteen or fifteen steps to the top, like a double-decker bus for the Flintstones. Too far south for an ice sheet, the Giant's

Brimham Rocks, Nidderdale, Yorkshire.

Rock on a rocky sea ledge at Porthleven, Cornwall is thought to have been dropped by a giant or an iceberg.

Rocks are named all around the coast, no doubt by mariners with a keen eye for danger and a need for landmarks. In Northumberland, where Old Norse words are in everyday use, *car(r)* and *bus* appear frequently, as in Oxcar, Jenny Bells Carr and the Bus of the Burn. Ancient peoples here felt the presence of rocks so keenly that they carved many of them remarkably; some five hundred examples of concentric and cup-and-ring patterns still exist. Northumberland has the definitive collection of five-thousand-year-old low-relief rock carvings, from a boulder in Powburn Quarry to the whaleback of sandstone near Roughting Linn waterfall, Milfield.

Hidden in the Forest of Dean, near Staunton, lies the Suck Stone, a massive wedge of rock sixty feet across, perhaps fourteen hundred tons. On the Derbyshire gritstone there are some great residual blocks, such as the Cat Stone and the Andle Stone on Stanton Moor; the Cork Stone has hand and foot holds for anyone with no tendency to vertigo. There is a characteristic look about millstone grit, amplified in the gritstone of Brimham Rocks in Nidderdale, Yorkshire, where rocks covering sixty acres stand proud in a labyrinthine group rather than spread along an edge. With names such as Dancing Bear, the Yoke of Oxen, Eagle and the Devil's Anvil, they have been variously described as *'indescribable'* in their '*multiform singularity*' and as '*the most outlandish assemblage of rugged curiosities*'. Here you can read the edge of an ancient sea where coarse sand was dropped at angles according to the flow of currents. After eons of burial and compaction the rock found itself naked before the sand-filled winds of a cold desert, which helped to etch the bedding planes and joints. In an animistic culture this would be a natural sacred place.

Natural 'logging' or logan stones had long been held in awe because they could be rocked. Occasional perched blocks transported by ice have this property, but more are the result of differential erosion of naturally stacking rock, found particularly in the gritstone of the Pennines and on the granite tors of Devon and Cornwall. Sadly for the vandals of today, many were unseated by Victorian visitors. The Logan Rock near Porthcurno in Cornwall was pushed so hard that it actually fell onto the beach below in 1824. Its importance in attracting visitors was so great that the locals insisted that it be replaced by the naval officer whose overzealousness had caused it to fall. He is remembered in the local pub sign.

ROOKERIES

Rookeries can be centuries old. The large, bulky nests high in the tree-tops are renewed by the same birds year after year. There may be only twenty or so nests, but there can be as many as several thousand. Rookeries are most welcome landmarks; near Stockbridge in Hampshire they occupy the tops of an avenue leading to a country house – there is a saying that rooks breed only where there is money.

Since the demise of the elm, their preferred tree, they have successfully moved to oak and ash, and sometimes sycamore, beech, limes, horse chestnut and Scots and Monterey pines. They have even been seen nesting at the top of a pylon near the M5 motorway junction at Warndon, Worcestershire.

Ranmoor Cliffe rookery, in the leafy western suburbs of Sheffield, has been recorded by the Sheffield Bird Study Group for the past forty years. It is a thriving colony with about two hundred nests in pine and broad-leaved trees growing on the slope of an old quarry, and is unusual to be situated in such a built-up area. Chris Stride's website records the following: '*The spectacle that draws most attention to the rookery is the flocking, visible (and audible) at dusk and dawn. This behaviour is most frequently observed during the summer evenings as the rooks fly in from a day spent feeding in the fields of the Mayfield valley. Some gather first in the tall tree on Gladstone Road, opposite the entrance to Graham Road, others on lamp-posts in the area, rather than returning directly to the rookery. Then they take to the air, begin to circle, and are soon joined by others to form a large and noisy black cloud. Every so often one breaks from the formation and dives from the air before resuming its swirling flight path. For country folk, these displays (known as tompoking, or making pancheons) used to indicate the onset of bad weather.*' Local people are appreciative: '*We absolutely love having the rooks around. From our dining table we can see them on summer evenings returning to the rookery and wheeling round – a wonderful sight. They really make you feel that you are somewhere other than in the suburb of a large city.*'

Mark Cocker, the closest and most lyrical of all rook watchers, describes their daily journeys in Norfolk, from their feeding places to their roosts, which can be as far as 27 miles away. '*As they stream towards me across the Yare floodplain there is the usual rich, plangent, drawn-out cawing, which echoes in this vast space … But mingled with these notes is a far wider range of soft, sometimes gull-like mewing sounds that rise on occasion into an almost yodelling sweetness. Then the jackdaws chip in with their snipped, dog-like yapping. It is a wonderful cacophony and it continues for about thirty minutes, as the birds* stream to their regular roost in oak stands near the hamlet of Buckenham. During that time I count about three thousand birds heading north across the river.'

There are a number of place and field names associated with rooks, but far more common is the name Rookery Farm. Mark Cocker has discovered more of these around Topcroft in East Anglia than in any other part of the country.

The Rooks, Lewes's football team, was called after the town's many rookeries. John Chaplin, chairman of the Lewes Tree Group, told us that 'the loss of elms, and we had many in the town, has caused the main rookery at Elm Grove, Southover High Street, to move along the street into sycamore and younger elm in front of Southover House. In that rookery there are now 25 active nests, over half of which have to be rebuilt each year.' In Eastgate Street there are seventeen nests in a two-hundred-year-old horse chestnut.

Rooks are widespread, often confused with their black corvid cousins, crows. The expression 'as the crow flies' really refers to rooks, which tend to fly in straight lines. Crows are more solitary, and rooks have a white patch around their beaks, which is the easiest way to distinguish them. They suffered from the effects of agricultural intensification and pesticide use in the 1960s and 1970s. They are now making a good recovery, but have not reached their pre-war numbers, and they continue to decline in the South East and Greater Manchester.

> … when the last rook
> Beat its straight path along the dusky air
> Homewards, I blest it!

SAMUEL TAYLOR COLERIDGE,
from 'This Lime-tree Bower My Prison'

SCULPTURES

Queen Victoria was one of the few women to sit on plinths in our cities. Most public works of art were extensions of classical sculpture – men/ gods on high. During the past two decades things have really changed. There has been a recognition that art can be and do much more radical things, helping us better to know and enjoy our surroundings and adding to the identity of places. Elisabeth Frink brought us horses on the ground at Piccadilly, London and martyrs walking among us in Dorchester. In the centre of Birmingham the fountains, steps and scattered sculptures offer the feeling of being in an open-air art gallery.

Around Drewsteignton in Devon subtle sculptures surprise along walks across the fields and hills. Peter Randall-Page worked to draw our gaze into the heart of a granite boulder, to the workings of a spring, to the simplicity of a drystone wall. Antony Gormley's sculptures work on both

'Angel of the North', Gateshead, County Durham.

monumental and intimate scales. His 'Angel of the North', 65 feet high by the A1, marks the entrance to Tyneside, celebrates local engineering skills and has offered itself as an icon for the North East; in the crypt of Winchester Cathedral, Hampshire a contemplative man stands unexpectedly up to his knees in water. 'Willow Man' by Serena de la Hey is a large figure running on the Somerset Levels near the M5, who tells of the culture of osier growing in a completely new form.

Early experiments by the Forestry Commission in giving young sculptors a massive canvas and endless materials in the Grizedale Forest, Lancashire began with David Nash creating 'Running Table'. Like the Forest of Dean in Gloucestershire, which followed its lead, it draws thousands of visitors willing to wander in search of art, perchancing on the wonders of the forest as they do.

Not at first seeming like an artistic endeavour, Andy Goldsworthy has been rebuilding sheep-folds in Cumberland and Westmorland. At Mungrisdale the land was cleared of great boulders, which now crowd around and hide the drystone sheep-fold as if pressing to get in. Drystone cones have been made for pinfolds in Bolton, Brough, Crosby, Outhgill, Raisbeck and Warcop, as guardians, each using the stone of the place. At Casterton there are sixteen small, square folds, following the Fellfoot Droves, each holding a large boulder. At Underbarrow near Kendal two folds encircle boulders through which planted rowan trees are growing – a memorial for the farmers who had to cope with the outbreak of foot-and-mouth disease. When the trees were planted late in 2001, Andy Goldsworthy said: '*The planting of any tree is a gesture of optimism and renewal – growing out of stone in the protective embrace of a sheep-fold will I hope give that gesture a potent mix of feelings – hardship, struggle, renewal, fragility, precariousness and strength. I could think of no better work on my part that could articulate the emotional struggle that has taken place for those living in badly affected areas during this intensely difficult time.*'

Plymouth city council charged Gordon Young with the task of giving identity to a ten-mile coast path to '*stop people getting lost, and we want it a bit interesting!'* So, from little fishes in the pavement to Brunel's Spanner, lettered railings to telegraph code words, a cross-section of the Eddystone lighthouse to a float bench – a red-and-white-striped old metal float with a seat hung along its side – you make your way round the edge of the city through artefacts and quotations, which offer glimpses of the composting of history in this place, much of it offered by local people. This and his wordy Cursing Stone and Reiver Pavement in the middle of Carlisle, Cumberland show how imagination, collaboration and quality can transform the feel of a place: they speak volumes.

SHEEP

The medieval and Elizabethan endowment of sheep can be seen in the glorious churches of East Anglia, the beautiful barns of the Cotswolds, the walls of Wensleydale, Yorkshire. The importance of sheep that can look after themselves on the fells and hills, that know their place, may be less obvious. Hill sheep are taught by their elders in the herd where to eat in the morning in May, where to seek shelter from frost, where to find water. Intimate knowledge of a territory, a daily round, shifting with season and weather, is passed down through the flock, and the shepherds. Hefting is one name given to this, the equivalent of a London taxi driver 'doing The Knowledge'. Flocks of sheep of the same breed make up hefted herds, which, all together on a mountain, make up the hirsel. It is illegal to remove the entire hirsel. The loss of animals to disease and economic volatility is a disaster for the culture of the sheep, as well as the people, because it takes generations for knowledge to be relearned.

The other great legacy is the extraordinary range of breeds, each originally developed by human as well as natural selection to survive well and produce most under conditions specific to the Dorset Downs, or the Cheviots, or Romney Marsh in Kent. Despite two centuries of convergent breeding, 65 named breeds still exist in Britain, for wool or meat or milk, and some are being used for conservation grazing. Many have such an intimacy with their sheep-walks that the quality of their meat and milk reflects this. The earliest sheep were shepherded here in neolithic times; the Vikings brought their own, as did some of the medieval monks. The Limestone breed was described by Robert Wallace as having evolved '*from time immemorial*' on the dry, precipitous slopes, from the Westmorland limestones to the White Peak in Derbyshire; it did poorly on boggy land. Close by, and in contrast, the Derbyshire Gritstone has survived. It was named as a breed on 15 October 1906, having been bred pure for the previous hundred years as the Dale o' Goyt (the Goyt valley runs towards Manchester).

One of our hardiest sheep, the Herdwick is native to the Fells of north Lancashire, Westmorland and Cumberland. So called because flocks were 'let' to a herdsman in lieu of wages, one story asserts that a wrecked ship from the Armada let some of its forebears ashore; another suggests that a Norwegian ship brought people and sheep from the north. There is variety within the Herdwicks themselves. In the lower lands the sheep are larger, with more and softer wool. The smallest, hardiest and healthiest survive on the fells, with scant eating and a real knowledge of the weather – they are said to foresee the approach of snow. Tall walls are a feature of their landscape, since they can easily jump six feet.

The *Shepherd's Guides*, started in the early nineteenth century, show the 'lug' or ear identifications. Caz Graham says: '*The guides are basically pictures of rather stylised sheep, with huge ears showing the individual marks that are cut out of each ear by different farmers. Each flock has its own mark, so that if sheep go missing on the fells ... they'll get back to their rightful owner ... The guides are updated every twenty years or so and the new one for the Lake District is going to have the new Defra flock numbers included and it's also going to be on the internet.*'

Ancient grazing rights exist in different landscapes; in the Forest of Dean, Gloucestershire the 'sheep badgers', who have rights to run sheep in the forest, are fighting to maintain their traditions.

Blue Faced Leicester.

Cheviot.

Clun Forest.

Derbyshire Gritstone.

Devon Longwool.

Herdwick.

Wensleydale.

Dorset Horn.

Creative farmers and producers of organic meat, sheep's milk and cheese are driving patches of resurgence, despite complex problems in the aftermath of overstocking and foot-and-mouth disease, and in the face of global markets. The endangered sheep breeds have their champions, but there needs to be a wider recognition of the importance of maintaining their genetic variegation and sustaining the culture, the everyday working knowledge, of the people who keep them.

STEPPING-STONES

Strategically placed boulders to enable foot travellers to stay dry, stepping-stones are such practical things. Yet to come across them brings great pleasure, especially when they have been worn by centuries of boots. Known as hipping stones in the North, the sturdy, rectangular stones over the Ribble at Stainforth, Yorkshire display this hollowing, as does the more random line that challenges the river Wharfe by Bolton Abbey. Also in Yorkshire, at Gargrave, beside an old ford across the river Aire, the stepping-stones, round and fresh, are a magnet for children. Masham town council commissioned Alan Ayers to make sculptures along the footpaths around town; only when crossing a fluctuating stream do you become aware that the stones are carved. Across the stream behind the main streets in Bruton, Somerset uneven stones offer short cuts.

STILES

Took a walk in the fields saw an old wood stile taken away from a favourite spot which it had occupied all my life the posts were overgrown with ivy and it seemed so akin to nature and the spot where it stood as tho it had taken it on lease for an undisturbed existence it hurt me to see it was gone for my affections claim a friendship with such things.

JOHN CLARE, from his Journal, September 1824

The most practical of artefacts attract our ingenuity and our affections. All over the country stiles of innumerable variations were and are still being devised to allow people to climb over hedges and walls into fields without letting sheep, cattle or even motorbikes follow them. The availability of stone, wood and metal reinforces the differences, but so does use and age, idiosyncrasy and tradition.

Some of the oldest are found in Cornwall, especially in West Penwith, where small fields are enclosed by huge, ancient hedge banks of earth and granite boulders, often topped by bushes. There is a sense of accumulation over generations and that many makeshift repairs have been made. Between 1997 and 2000 the Gerrans and Porthscatho Old Cornwall Society surveyed the old stiles in the parishes of St Gerrans, Philleigh and St Just and found three main types: the cattle stile, sheep stile and coffin stile, and variations.

The cattle stile through the hedge bank is the most simple and common, the airy gap spanned by a thin high stone (the shape of a lintel) with one or more stones as steps to it on either side; alternatively the stone steps lead up to a solid slab. One, at Treloan Farm, has a locally typical cart axle across the top; it is Grade II-listed.

The sheep or step stile involves a number of stones projecting from the face of a stone hedge, rising up and over each side. A granite slab sits on top of the 'hedge', which can be as wide as four feet. Where the coursing is of vertical slate, large granite steps can look rather ungainly.

The coffin stile is an early form of cattle grid, with deep stone slats or 'treads' sometimes placed over a shallow pit, and was used to replace gates into a churchyard. One at St Just has a shelf for the coffin to rest on at both sides.

If in Cornwall you have to be nimble; in Derbyshire and the Yorkshire Dales you need to be slender to get through the squeeze stiles. At their simplest just two large slabs of stone make a V shape through the stone wall, the gap narrow enough to deter sheep and cattle. Sometimes the stone slabs are roughly hewn, but they can also be beautifully tooled, as at Callow and Kirk Ireton in Derbyshire and Flockton Moor, Yorkshire. In Derbyshire the curvaceous profiles of limestone stoops or slabs in Monyash give more space for feet; there is even more elaborate keyhole shaping in the sandstone stoops at Newhaven.

Sometimes the stones are offset to allow a shuffle through, with one squared or wedge-shaped stone in front of the other, as at Twiston, Lancashire. Other variations include step-over squeezers and straight-sided stiles, with or without steps. Quite different are the elegant steps made from over-long throughstones protruding either side to allow escalation over walls, which are typical of parts of the Yorkshire moors and Dales; some may date from the seventeenth century, as at Malham.

Occasional mounting-block-type stiles lead into a churchyard; else-where, for example at Ribchester, Lancashire, elaborately wide steps might lead up and over a low, vertical, gravestone-like slab. In Somerset, at Farrington Gurney, two thinly cut stones elegantly curve away from each other like angel's wings and, just beyond, a vertical iron bar topped with a curly ended 'T' stops small animals getting through.

Simple, wooden step-over stiles predominate in hedged country. Near Burwash in Sussex a charming, curved, wooden 'V', with a piece of wood nailed as a cross-bar and a step on short posts, acts as a makeshift squeezer stile and has probably been there for years. At Coombes in Sussex and Lacock in Wiltshire wood has been shaped to resemble stone

Cornish grid stile.

Wooden stile.

Squeeze stile, Great Longstone, Derbyshire.

Stone steps, Cleveland, Yorkshire.

slabs for squeezer stiles. Tall, wooden ladder stiles have spread across the Pennines and the Lake District in recent decades to help walkers climb over the high walls.

Stiles made in metal are among the most elegant, but may say little of locality save that here was an estate or park. Iron fence steps, ladders and kissing gates were available from Victorian catalogues. Iron ladders with a great circle for handrails are good for clearing high deer fences, for example at Horton, Lancashire, or lower, metal estate fencing, at Dubwath, Cumberland. Inverted bottled-shaped metal squeeze stiles are *'typical of those found around the Bath area. It is called "The Fat Man's Agony"'*, according to Michael Roberts. Those made from iron pipes for the water authority at Monkton Combe, Somerset have a workaday appropriateness. A metal scissor stile into the churchyard at Duntisbourne Rouse,

Gloucestershire neatly folds to one side to let the walker through. Mechanical turnstiles persist in a few locations, as on Lindisfarne, Northumberland.

Along the river Parrett in Somerset Keith Rand has made wineglass-shaped oak squeeze stiles, demonstrating that sculptors and craftspeople have creative ideas to offer, at their best when the brief demands a new and subtle look at local distinctiveness.

SWIMMING PLACES

> *Oh, many a time have I, a five years' child,*
> *In a small mill-race severed from his stream,*
> *Made one long bathing of a summer's day;*
> *Basked in the sun, and plunged and basked again*
> *Alternate, all a summer's day …*

WILLIAM WORDSWORTH, from 'Bathing'

Most rivers have their special spots – deep pools or old mill-ponds known to locals, where farmers turn a blind eye to benign play. Wild swimming, as Roger Deakin calls it, clings on: '*Often there's a shingle river beach near a bridge or in the elbow of an oxbow bend, or a deep pool with a submerged ladder in the bank. And the classic sign known to all unofficial bathers: a dangling, knotted rope for swinging out like Tarzan, and letting go.*'

People have been swimming in the river Frome, Wiltshire at Farleigh Weir since at least the 1500s, and from the 1930s Farleigh Swimming Club, with seventeen hundred members, has enjoyed bathing here in a pool by a tree-lined water-meadow.

Yet no rivers are designated bathing waters under the European Bathing Water Directive. When asked why, the Environment Agency replied: '*The Agency does not encourage informal swimming in rivers by members of the general public.*' But the aspiration should be that all rivers are clean enough to swim in, simple streams safe to play in and springs proudly cared for by all of us.

'*Today's swimmers … are herded into chemically treated pools that simulate nature but have the wildness carefully filtered out, the "real thing" is treated with shameless disrespect*,' writes Deakin, whose book *Waterlog* is about not just '*our profound disconnection from natural waters*' but our insidious distancing from nature, which compounds ignorance, disrespect and bad decision-making. The suggested closing, by the Corporation of London, of the three swimming ponds on London's Hampstead Heath to the Hampstead Heath Winter Swimming Club was for some the final straw, and success-fully challenged in the High Court. Local people hold dear the free right to swim at their own risk in daylight hours in soft, untainted water all year, in the spring-fed men's, ladies' and mixed ponds, among kingfishers, swans and ducklings.

Some hardy people swim every day, some join in at the challenging moment of Christmas or New Year's Day, as in Suffolk with the Walbers-wick Shiverers – '*a group of friends who exercise their right to insanity by plunging into the North Sea each Christmas Day*'. The Christmas Day race is the highlight for members of the Serpentine Swimming Club (formed in 1864) in Hyde Park, London, most of whom take a pre-work swim here daily.

TERRIERS

Terriers are unique to Britain – all the terrier breeds originate here. Their name derives from *terra*, earth, and they have been bred since the 1650s to pursue animals that live underground – which 'go to earth' when chased. Many counties had their own breed of terrier, each with practical working skills.

In Cumberland the '*square-built*' fell or Lakeland type of terrier was bred to accompany foot followers and, according to D. Brian Plummer, '*put to ground to kill a fox*', rather than flush it out, when the fox was seen simply as vermin with no potential for 'sport'.

Airedales are thought to have been the result of mating bull terriers with otter hounds to produce a large ratting (and otter-hunting) terrier capable of working the banks of the river Aire in Yorkshire. In the 1800s John Hulme from Manchester crossed a terrier derived from the old English black-and-tan type with a whippet to improve its ratting and rabbiting skills. The result was the handsome, smooth-haired black-and-tan terrier, later known as the Manchester terrier. It is now becoming rare.

The Bedlington terrier, formerly Rothbury terrier, which was bred by Gypsies and miners from Rothbury Forest, Northumberland, is a combination of lurcher and a terrier brought by nail-makers from the South. Once called the Gypsy dog, used to hunt badgers, rabbits and otters, it was the poacher's favourite, and miners used it down the pit to kill rats. In someone's arms it looks remarkably like a curly-coated lamb with Roman nose and drooping ears. Yet on their own feet they are distinguished by a roached back and hanging tail, perhaps a little like hairy whippets; meeting seven of them – the Rotherview and Toffset Bedlingtons, fashionably clipped – on the beach at Exmouth, Devon on the day before the Paignton Show confirmed that they look like nothing else.

The plucky Border terrier was formerly known as the Reedwater or Coquetdale terrier. Described by Veronica Heath as the '*canine aristocrats of the north east*', with their small, otter-shaped heads and wiry coats, they were bred to join the hunt for foxes in the border country between Scotland and England. The Scottish borders have also been the home, for four hundred years, of the good-natured, long-haired, long-backed and short-legged Dandie Dinmont terrier, or tinker's dog, which was bred for killing stoats and rats.

The short-legged, wiry coated Norfolk and Norwich terriers differ slightly: the Norwich has prick ears and the Norfolk 's are dropped. The Norwich was popular with hunt-loving students at Cambridge in the late 1800s, but now is becoming rare.

Airedale.

Bedlington.

Border.

Lakeland.

Manchester.

Norwich.

'Each English county once had its own fox terrier,' Dr Bruce Fogle wrote, 'the genes of the extinct White Cheshire and Shropshire Terrier are probably still present in this breed, together with those of the Beagle.' The smooth-haired and the more popular wire-haired terriers, with their thicker legs and dense whiskers, were bred for flushing foxes.

The vicar of Swimbridge and Landkey in north Devon, Reverend Jack Russell, spent most of his time from 1832 to 1884 trying to 'improve the working Fox terrier' for hunting. In other words, making it 'steady from riot' and not tempted to chase other quarry. He produced a type of white, wire-haired terrier with legs long enough to enable it to keep up with the horses – the Parson Jack Russell. The more numerous and more variable Jack Russell, the most popular of all terriers, has slightly shorter legs and can be smooth or wire-haired.

The sturdy Staffordshire bull terrier has shorter legs than the bull terrier and a different-shaped head, coming from an English White terrier and bulldog cross. It was originally bred for bull baiting and dog fighting, which was popular in the Walsall and Bloxwich areas of the west Midlands.

The popularity of the terrier is confirmed by the variety of breeds, which number more than any other type of dog. The first terrier show, organised by Charles Cruft in 1886, was so successful that it was later enlarged to include other breeds.

During the past few years some of the old breeds have begun to lose their popularity, such as the Sealyham. Registrations with the Kennel Club for the diminutive Yorkshire terrier, which was once stuffed into the pockets of West Riding miners for ratting work, declined by more than sixty per cent between 1993 and 2002. Two of the original breeds – the black and tan and the white English terrier – together with the Cheshire, Devonshire, Shropshire and Suffolk terriers and other localised breeds, such as the Redesdale, have been absorbed into other breeds or become extinct.

VERGES

The green estate alongside Britain's roads covers some 523,000 acres – the size of Surrey. In pre-enclosure England highways and their verges were part of the common land of the manor, forming a valuable resource – sheep still graze along the unfenced roadsides of the uplands. Along droves, verges sustained livestock on their way to market; in south-east Norfolk 'narrow' or 'street' commons and greens are visible remnants of a linear network of grazing verges. Road verges might be wide for other reasons, too: in the clay-rich areas ways grew wider as travellers struggled to avoid the ruts. Early nineteenth-century estate maps show cigar-shaped fields lining the roads, as enterprising small farmers claimed bits of the verge for themselves.

Traditionally cut for hay, grazed, or scythed by parish 'lengthmen', verges are now refuges for ancient hay-meadow flowers, such as dyer's greenwood and spiny restharrow – both are more likely to be found by a road than in their original home in the fields – as well as cowslip, knapweed, rockrose and hay-rattle. Primrose banks are eagerly watched out for, orchid verges jealously guarded. When cow-parsley blooms, motorists know that summer has arrived. Wilding apple trees, from discarded cores, bring welcome blossom and fruit – their boughs unpruned and ungrazed often reach the ground.

Across the chalklands of the South, roads are edged with downland refugees; in the Weald ancient sunken lanes through steep sandstone banks shelter a rich woodland flora of delicate mosses and ferns. Eroded over hundreds of years by generations of feet, hooves, cartwheels and water, these hollow ways have acquired strong characters. On the Surrey greensand their verges carry some of the county's rarest hawkweeds and orchids. Quiet Herefordshire lanes sport primrose, stitchwort, bluebell, red campion and, later, perhaps harebells. Devon lanes add bastard balm; those in Gloucestershire's Severn vale support lady's smock.

On the Lizard Peninsula in Cornwall trackways with hedge banks harbour wild madder, navelwort and three-cornered leek. Puddles in cart-tracks across the Cornish moorland support a rare and tiny rush – its life cycle depends upon a vehicle using the ancient track just once or twice a year. Perennial flax is a good sign of a Roman road on chalk or limestone verges; it grows along Ermine Street and the A11, just north of Stump Cross, a 'Romanised' stretch of the Icknield Way marking the Essex/Cambridgeshire boundary.

Not long ago the Highways Agency routinely seeded new road verges with imported 'wildflower mixtures' – a practised eye can still spot the bold ox-eye daisies from eastern Europe along many a town bypass. In recent years, however, the best road schemes have been 'greened' with locally sourced stock. In places, more enlightened regimes are also replacing weed-killer spraying or mechanical mowing at the wrong times of year. In east Sussex sixteen miles of road verge are marked with special 'wildlife verge' posts, monitored by volunteers and managed for birds, butterflies and bumblebees; three such verges harbour spiked rampion, found almost nowhere else in the country.

VILLAGES

What we love about villages was captured by H.J. Massingham during his sojourn through *English Downland*: '*How effortlessly each of them preserves a particular identity of its own! The smaller they are, the more isolated, the more isolated the flintier. The richer they are in little undemonstrative mannerisms of tile-hanging and weather-boarding, and the readier to avail themselves of the immemorial material of the chalk at their doors, the more vital is their personality ... They are as true to their downs as are the ringed citadels of those hill-people slaughtered by their founders.*'

Villages seem old, by virtue of their materials, which are 'true' to their place, and because of the way they sit in the land and have done for perhaps hundreds of years. Capitals of their parishes, villages are small settlements, generally with church, perhaps with pub, shop and chapel, although increasingly these have become residences.

They have many origins, rooted in economic and cultural activities as well as physical fortune. The reasons for their existence may be long gone, perhaps even the spring or ford, mineral wealth, agriculture, fishing, certainly the garrison, are lost. Some cling on despite being overwhelmed by a major road or being enmeshed in development; some, on the other hand, revel in being seen as villages in the city – Dulwich, Greenwich and Hampstead, for example, in London.

Villages are typical of the lower lands; in the old open field areas of the Midlands, especially, nucleated villages predominate. In the uplands the patterns tend towards hamlets and scattered farms. Many village settlements are probably older even than their names suggest, and most carry names from Anglo-Saxon or Romano-British times. Observers continue to mine the names, situations and shapes for clues. Their morphology is infinitely varied, but broad patterns can be seen: long, thin street villages, nucleated villages, square or green villages gathered around small or large commons, and all manner of squatted or loosely scattered settlements.

Ashmore, high on the chalk in Dorset, may be a Romano-British settlement still clustered round its pond. Long Melford in Suffolk states its case, but Combe Martin, Devon claims to be the longest village in England on its Parish Map. It has extended down the narrow valley for more than a mile to the sea. Straggling villages along Norfolk rivers are the result of each house needing a long, thin holding to link the transport potential of both watercourse and street.

Estate villages comprise buildings eerily of the same moment – sanitised, unreal visions of the picturesque. Some were the result of clearing the view. Milton Abbas village in Dorset replaced the market town of more than a hundred houses that was removed out of sight of the manor by Baron Milton in the late eighteenth century. Its detached and semi-detached white, thatched houses formally front a single street with open lawns. Edensor, Derbyshire, with its elaborately chimneyed and strangely diverse villas, was designed by Paxton to leave Chatsworth House an open prospect.

Villages serving single industries spontaneously grew around mine, pottery or brick works, as along the Medway in Kent. Some were planned and orderly, as at Ironville in Derbyshire. Villages notable for houses with extensive upper windows speak of home weavers, as at Golcar, Yorkshire, and frame knitters, in Ockbrook, Derbyshire.

Model villages emerged to offer better living conditions first for agricultural and then industrial workers. Paternalism and philanthropy made for tied workers but better living conditions, too. Enlightened industrialists, especially Quakers, made their utopian ideals a reality. In Worcestershire Cadbury's model village of Bournville, with its low-density detached housing, gardens and greens, influenced Joseph Rowntree of York to build New Earswick in 1902/3. He sought to address the social and physical problems of poverty, offering independence as well as health, air and light. Reckitt created his Garden Village in Hull; Lever Port Sunlight on the Wirral; Crittall made Silver End in Essex and Vickers built Vickerstown in Barrow-in-Furness, Lancashire.

New villages now appear out of desperate national housing policies and pressure from house builders, few of which work hard to add to quality and local distinctiveness. A growing movement interested in self-build, community making and/or eco-credentials is inventing new aesthetics and dynamics, from the Lightmoor self-build community in Shropshire to BedZed (architect Bill Dunster) in Sutton, Surrey, which provides housing, work space and community facilities for a hundred people.

'Real' villages evolve, adapt, change, reinvent vitality. The challenge we now face is ensuring that places are neither coated in aspic nor overwhelmed, their authenticity eroded by tidiness, absence or imposed housing targets.

WAYSIDE & BOUNDARY CROSSES

Wild moors and stone crosses keep company with one another. Striding across Dartmoor, medieval granite crosses link the abbeys of Buckland, Buckfast and Tavistock that fringe the moor. Horn's Cross, Mount Misery Cross and Siward's (or Nun's) Cross are just three waymarks along the Monk's Path. Some of the 150 or so crosses are reckoned to be more than a thousand years old; many have been lost and some found again. Mark stones were often put up to guide travellers across difficult and remote terrain. Others are boundary markers or more recently erected memorials or commemorative stones.

Chapel Amble Cross, St Kew, Cornwall.

Malo Cross, Saltergate, Yorkshire.

Bennet's Cross, Dartmoor, Devon.

Of the many remnants and simple crosses, such as Old Ralph and Fat Betty, on the Yorkshire Moors, one of the finest is Lilla Cross on Fylingdales Moor, believed to stand over the grave of the chief minister who died for his king, Edwin of Northumbria, in AD 625.

Cornwall is known for its ancient granite crosses. More than four hundred complete crosses have been recorded, and perhaps two hundred bits and bases. Most of the wayside crosses and boundary crosses are on the West Penwith and Bodmin moors. Wayside crosses mark the footpaths and tracks to parish churches, monasteries, chapels, holy wells and pilgrim routes. On coffin paths crosses were erected at the places where coffin bearers rested. At St Clether on Bodmin Moor a round or wheel-headed cross shows where it is safe to ford the river Inny.

Boundary crosses demarcate parish glebe land and perhaps monastic boundaries and church sanctuaries. The Cross in Hand on Tregonetha Downs marks the place where three parish boundaries meet. The parish of St Buryan in West Penwith, with a sanctuary extending beyond the walls of the churchyard, contains the greatest number of old crosses in the county. Most of the wayside and boundary crosses are wheel-headed, some carved with the figure of Christ; some have a Latin cross in relief painted with limewash. Holed wheel crosses are found throughout the Cornish moorlands; many have lost their base stones and shafts.

Some crosses have been found in hedge banks, with shafts used as gateposts. A number have been found by researching field names: two fields called Cross Park revealed previously undiscovered stones.

Most of the crosses are dated between the ninth and thirteenth centuries. The Longcross in the parish of St Endellion is one of four very early Christian inscribed stones in Cornwall that display the chi-rho monogram. It also has an inscription in Latin and Ogham.

WILDFLOWERS

Our passive appreciation of wild plants lies in deep contrast to our fore-bears' practical, everyday knowledge and need of them. Working wisdom about plants was mixed with superstitions and inherited associations with magic and special powers. A culture of plant lore flourished, some of which persists, from using feverfew against headaches to not taking hawthorn blossom into the house because it brings bad luck.

Formal knowledge took a step forward in 1551 when William Turner from Morpeth, Northumberland wrote the first part of his *New Herball*. Woodcuts borrowed from Bavarian physician Leonhard Fuchs provided

accurate portrayals of the plants to aid identification. Katrina Porteous says: '*This book was a landmark in botany and medicine. For the first time, physicians were able to read in their own language, English, an original study of the plants vital to their profession.*' He was criticised: '*Now … every man, nay every old wife, will presume, not without the murder of many, to practise Physik,*' one detractor claimed. In 1597 John Gerard's more famous *Herball* was published and many others followed.

The first *Flora of the British Isles* and the initial County Flora – of Cambridgeshire – were compiled by John Ray in 1660. Distinguished amateur and professional botanists, including many Victorian clergymen, have since compiled comprehensive County Floras. We have also produced some fine botanical illustrators, such as the Reverend William Keeble Martin, who have given us a good picture of the treasury of wild plants we had. H.C. Watson pioneered a more systematic method of cataloguing plants, with distribution maps, in *Cybele Britannica* (1847) and *Topographical Botany* (1883). Now we have the technology to map precisely what plants we have left, but not the will, it seems, to conserve them.

In *The Englishman's Flora* (1958) the writer and poet Geoffrey Grigson explored our cultural relationship with plants, including local and vernacular names that give clues to their uses and our attitudes towards them. For example, one of the field poppy's local names, headache, refers to people's fears that smelling a poppy would bring one on. This connects with other names – thunderbolt, thunderflower and thundercup warned children that picking the flower may presage a storm.

Grigson's work has been importantly amplified by *Flora Britannica*, Richard Mabey's *tour de force*, which brings together contemporary botany with continuing everyday familiarity with plants, incorporating information sent by hundreds of local correspondents and using colour photographs instead of botanical illustrations.

Ox-eye daisy.

The geological and topographical complexity of England is mirrored by an intricate distribution of wild plants. Even within a single parish the range of habitats offers many niches – from wet valley bottoms to exposed hilltops, from coast to heath and woodland, even from the south to the north side of a wall.

That wildflowers thrive in thin, unpromising soils and in difficult conditions is their virtue and their undoing. Put down fertiliser and the plants are soon crowded out by vigorous grasses and crops; herbicides complete the affront. Yet man and nature had worked together for hundreds of years, giving us rich flora in arable fields and continuous grassland. One old hay meadow can contain as many as 150 different plants. The unnatural, mono-tonal green of the fields signals not only the loss of richness but also the loss of variegation, the failure of the local patois of the wild.

Brutal forms of intensive agriculture have eliminated most wildflowers from the hay meadows, water-meadows and arable fields. The so-called arable 'weeds', hay rattle, corn cockle and corn marigold, are now very rare. Wetland plants continue to disappear fast, owing to widespread land-drainage schemes. Meadows of fritillaries used to be commonplace in river valleys of the South and East, now a handful remain. Even the resilient buttercups are becoming a less familiar spring spectacle.

Arguments for benign farming fell on deaf ears. The Department of the Environment's 'Countryside Survey 1993' reported that even the traditional reservoirs of wild plants, such as hedgerows, riverbanks and road verges, had suffered a loss in diversity even when not physically damaged. By 2004 a survey found that nearly a third of native British plants had significantly decreased in forty years, and in 2005 it was stated that one in five of our wildflowers is threatened with extinction.

The strategy of conservationists has been to safeguard key sites, both for research and so that plants can recolonise the surrounding areas when conditions improve. But there is danger in this approach. In some places these reserves have become vulnerable, isolated islands, surrounded by one crop and little else. Nothing can replace the familiar plants in their everyday landscapes, for us or for the security of the species. Parish Floras give us the scale on which to sense gain or loss, and are where real conservation should begin.

In Devon residents made a poster of the Flora of Chagford. It has beautiful illustrations of one hundred species found in the parish, from navelwort on the granite walls, tansy and cuckoo flower in the hedge-rows, bilberry on the moors, ragged robin in the marshy places, water crowfoot in the river and dog's mercury in the woods, to self-heal, catsear, devil's bit and field scabious in the meadows. While researching their Parish Map project they discovered a meadow that has never been ploughed or sprayed, which contains 46 species of flowering plant.

The Parish Mappers of Elham, Kent also discovered the richness of their chalk flora; in addition to their eight-by-four-foot painted Parish Map they have made a floral map, and they are now tackling the hard job of conserving what they have and creating the right conditions to enable wildflowers to return.

It is the common, not the rare, plants that characterise places and tell the seasons: snowdrops along Wiltshire streams, lesser celandine ('spring messenger') along the road verges, carpets of bluebells in Derbyshire's Derwent woods, white ramsons in Hampshire hedge bottoms, stretches of gorse across the Bagshot sands in Surrey, bilberry on the Pennine moors, the patriotic mix of red campion, stitchwort and bluebells along the deep lanes of Herefordshire, thrift along the Cornish coast – things we hope our grandchildren will take for granted.

WOODS

We have no wilderness, no expanses of wildwood, no great forests on the scale of northern Europe. What we do have are ancient woods, and they are the more precious because, as Oliver Rackham writes, '*For a thousand years England, at least, has had less woodland than most European countries and has taken correspondingly more care of its woods. By the thirteenth century* AD *woodland management was a fully-developed art with conservation as its chief objective.*' We and our woods have learned to live and work together, although there have been aberrations: voracious coniferisation and the loss of woodland skills in the twentieth century, for example.

This was predominantly a wooded land, and the remnants of ancient woodland present the richest of all habitats, from the flora, fauna and mycorrhizal fungi of their soils to the range of lichens, ferns, insects, birds and animals they support and the shrubs and flowers beneath them. We also have patches of wood pasture in parkland, where grazing with occasional trees has been the regime for hundreds of years.

Trees rarely gather as a single species, as in the yew wood of Kingley Vale in Sussex. Most enjoy one another's company, different assemblages typifying different ecological and conservation conditions. Oliver Rackham suggests at least 31 types of ancient woodland in England; George Peterken offered 58 ancient and semi-natural woodland types. They multiply within the broader groupings of ash-wych elm, ash-maple, hazel-ash, ash-lime, oak-lime, chestnut, birch-oak, alder, beech, hornbeam and elm.

Oaks are our most common woodland trees; sessile oak (*Quercus petraea*) predominates in the North and West uplands and pedunculate oak (*Quercus robur*) in the South and East. Birch now pops up anywhere; it is a hardy pioneer, enjoying the company of oak. Ash seeks out the limestones, from the Mendips in Somerset to the magnesian limestone in County Durham. Beech prefers chalk downs and wolds and the oolitic limestone of the Cotswolds; under its dark shadow little will grow, making it one of the most open woodlands in which to walk. Hornbeam is most comfortable in the Home Counties, and sweet chestnut sticks to the South on acid soils. Alder enjoys plashy places; it still dominates the Broads and wet parts of Breckland in Norfolk and, together with willow, borders the Cheshire meres. Wych elm makes for mixed woodland, especially in the North. Lime woods are found in Lincolnshire, but rarely elsewhere (although six thousand years ago lime was *the* lowland tree). Beneath the oaks and beech of the New Forest holly muscles in. Among the colours of the Wye valley in spring the white blossom of the wild cherry stands out. Box hangs on where it is dry and warm, as at Box Hill in Surrey, and the sparely scattered wild service tree usually indicates lime or clay.

To visit a favourite bluebell wood in spring or to explore the wood close by every day is a luxury with real benefits:

> *Who hath not felt the influence that so calms*
> *The weary mind in summers sultry hours*
> *When wandering thickest woods beneath the arms*
> *Of ancient oaks and brushing nameless flowers*

JOHN CLARE, from 'Wood Rides'

Woods make places. The abundance of woodland in Kent and Sussex is unexpected, so densely peopled are they. In Dorset the absence of woodland is equally surprising.

The Forestry Commission is changing its emphasis on discordant evergreens, which have dominated planting for three-quarters of a century, diminishing the personality and ecology of so much of our uplands and heaths. Over the next century it will '*persecute the conifer*' in favour of hardwood, carbon fixing, nature conservation, recreation and landscape.

Woods are always changing: expanding as grazing diminishes in the uplands, failing to regenerate as abundant deer eat saplings, contracting as development presses, degenerating as craft skills are lost. Lack of disturbance is important – ancient woodland and semi-natural woods may contain varieties of common species that have adapted to local conditions. But, as climate warms, droughts come more often, diseases

proliferate and storms threaten. The debate is on. Should we be planting other varieties of oak and chestnut, and species such as walnut, and
finally allowing that the sycamore is worth having? We all need to be
involved, it is our places that will be changing. And we must actively
work the patches of woodland around us, as well as planting more, for, as
W.H. Auden said, '*a culture is no better than its woods*'.

XANADU

The way we see our surroundings is a cultural phenomenon that shifts
and changes. The seventeenth century brought revolutions in scientific
and technological thought, which led to the expansion of industry, the
growth of cities and the drift to a mass society. In the eighteenth century
a ripple of reaction grew into a flood through the poets and artists of the
Romantic movement.

They began to express how they valued Nature for its spiritual power
rather than simple utility, in what Alasdair Clayre described as '*the new
genius that broke through at this moment, in the description of the landscape,
in the sense of communion with nature and in the feeling of close relationship with
all other living beings*'. They explored their sensibilities through emotion
and morality, expressing nostalgia for the loss of innocence and beauty.

Some of our greatest poets, including William Blake, Lord Byron,
John Clare, Samuel Taylor Coleridge, John Keats, Percy Bysshe Shelley
and William Wordsworth, added to the momentum.

The great poetic outburst of Romanticism, hardly vanquished by
T.S. Eliot and twentieth-century poetry, has influenced us all. Just as
Columbus did not 'discover' America, neither did the eighteenth-century
thinkers 'discover' beauty, or even 'the sublime' in the mountains, nor
for the first time see '*a World in a Grain of Sand*', but their words shifted
our cultural vision, sizing the canvas for others, including Turner and
Constable – '*Painting is but another word for feeling*'.

Coleridge spent much time in the West Country, exploring the importance of the Imagination and pioneering the transference of the experience of walking in the hills, in weather or by the sea into poetry. Exchanging visits with his good friends Dorothy and William Wordsworth in the Lake District, his own role was eclipsed by the work he influenced in William Wordsworth – the seminal poetry of *The Prelude*.

The vital role of detail and the particular to the poetic mind is nowhere more poignantly told than in this cautionary tale. Depressed and tired, Coleridge one day went for a long walk on his own, from his house at Nether Stowey in the Quantock Hills in Somerset. He had been reading *The Pilgrimage* – '*In Xanada did Cublai Can build a stately Pallace*' – by Samuel Purchas (1614), which clearly echoed in his mind. He was not well and stopped on the way, probably at the isolated Ash Farm.

Here, '*in a sort of Reverie brought on by two grains of Opium, taken to check a dysentery*', he began to compose a poem in his head:

> *In Xannadù did Cubla Khan*
> *a stately Pleasure Dome decree;*
> *Where ALPH, the sacred River, ran*
> *Thro caverns measureless to Man*
> *Down to a sunless Sea.*

His dreaming was broken by a knock at the door. Punctuation so profound that we shall never know what more Coleridge had to say, since later he could retrieve but 54 lines – the '*person on business from Porlock*' had interrupted the Muse. This fragment of poetry, exotic in inception as well as content, has nevertheless been tied by Richard Holmes to the '*erotic, magical geography of Culborne Combe seen from Ash Farm*'.

ZIGZAGS

Gilbert White, father of natural history, created a formal path through the beech trees from Selborne in the eighteenth century, as recounted by Richard Mabey: *'he built the famous zig zag up the Hanger, and at the top a hermitage in which to hold summer picnics'.*

But it was the Victorians who popularised the idea of the promenade, and with it the proliferation of paths negotiating steep slopes for the sheer enjoyment of finding a view. Londoners flocked to Box Hill in Surrey by railway in the nineteenth century and took pleasure in walking up the chalk Zig Zag. With the dominance of the car this has become a metalled road and is enjoyed as a challenge by drivers, as is Zig-Zag Hill in Dorset, which climbs thrillingly through ever-tightening chicanes up the chalk edge towards Ashmore.

Many seaside towns boast fine promenades overlooked by hotels and encouraging bracing walks in view of the sea. Bournemouth, a Victorian invention, masses its hotels along the cliff top, with winding walks and wind-blown pine trees. There is also a remarkable promenade along the undercliff, with beach huts, booths and breakwaters disappearing in perspective along the strand. Linking the upper walks and lower promenade are the chines and an array of zigzag paths, the bane of parents in search of leisure, the joy of little legs. The views are at each turn spectacular, with the Needles glistening from the Isle of Wight and Old Harry from the Isle of Purbeck.

Folkestone also has a high promenade, the Leas, the place to be seen in Edwardian times, backed by hotels, lawns and bandstand. From here you can drop straight down in the funicular Leas Lift, or via tortuous paths through fantastic artificial tunnels and caves, catching your breath on the way up in tucked-in shelters with fine views.

Short Bibliography & References
See *England in Particular* for fuller Bibliography

Introduction
Clifford, Sue and King, Angela (Eds). *Local Distinctiveness: Place Particularity and Identity*. Conference papers. Common Ground, 1993.
Alleys
Bebbington, G. *Street Names of London*. Batsford, 1972.
Geographers' A–Z London Atlas
Jones, Mark W. *A Walk around the Snickleways of York*. William Sessions, 1983.
Room, A. *The Street Names of England*. Paul Watkins, 1992.
Whitworth, A. *The A–Z of Whitby Yards*. Culva House, 2003.
Ancient Trees
Johnson, O. (Ed). *Champion Trees, The Tree Register*. Whittet Books, 2003.
Rackham, Oliver. *History of British Countryside*. Dent, 1986.
Arcades
Dixon, R. and Muthesius, S. *Victorian Architecture*. Thames and Hudson, 1985.
Lloyd, David W. *The Making of English Towns*. Gollancz, 1984.
Beachcombing
Gates, Phil. 'Country Diary'. *Guardian*, 7 November 2002.
Beating the Bounds
Hodgson's *History of Northumberland*. 1758.
Kightly, Charles. *The Customs and Ceremonies of Britain*. Thames and Hudson, 1986.
Averton Gifford Parish Map. 1992.
Bells & Bell-Ringing
Baker, Mary. *Folklore and Customs of Rural England*. David and Charles, 1974.

Camp, John. *In Praise of Bells*. Hale, 1988.
Strutt, Joseph. The *Sports and Pastimes of the People of England*. 1838.
Dartmoor Changes (CD). Aune Head Arts, 2005.
The Towers and Bells Handbook. The Towers and Belfries Committee of the Central Council of Church Bell Ringers, 1973.
Bluebells
Grigson, Geoffrey. *The Englishman's Flora*. Paladin, 1975.
Mabey, Richard. *Flora Britannica*. Chatto and Windus, 1996.
Marren, Peter. *Woodland Heritage*. David and Charles, 1990.
Cairns
Allen, Bob. *Escape to the Dales*. Michael Joseph, 1992.
Goldsworthy, Andy. *Sheepfolds*. Michael Hue-Williams Fine Art, 1996.
Wainwright, A. *Fellwalking with Wainwright*. Michael Joseph, 1984.
Canals
Hadfield, Charles and Boughey, Joseph. *Hadfield's British Canals*. Alan Sutton, 1998.
Jones, Barbara. *The Unsophisticated Arts*. The Architectural Press, 1951.
Churches
Atkinson, T.D. *Local Style in English Architecture*. B.T. Batsford, 1947.
Gilbert, O. *Lichens*. HarperCollins, 2000.
Jenkins, Simon. *England's Thousand Best Churches*. Penguin Books, 2000.
Morris, E. *Towers and Bells of Britain*. Robert Hale, 1955.

Clouds

Goethe, J.W. von. 'In Honour of Howard' (translated by Hüttner, Johann Christian and Soane, George). *London Magazine and Theatrical Inquisitor IV*, July 1821.

Hamblyn, R. *The Invention of Clouds*. Picador, 2001.

Shelley, Percy Bysshe. 'The Cloud'. *Prometheus Unbound: a Lyrical Drama in four acts, with other poems*. C. and J. Ollier, 1820.

Commons

Clayden, Paul. *Our Common Land*. Open Spaces Society, 2003.

Gould, Dennis. From *Greenham Common Blues*. Posterpoem, Green CND, 1982.

Stamp, D. and Hoskins, W.G. *The Common Lands of England and Wales*. Collins, 1963.

Williamson, T. and Bellamy, L. *Property and Landscape*. George Philip, 1987.

Cornish Pasties

Hall, Stephen. *The Cornish Pasty*. AGRE Books, 2001.

Harben, Philip. *Traditional Dishes of Britain*. The Bodley Head, 1953.

Trewin, Carol, and Woolfitt, Adam. *Gourmet Cornwall,* Alison Hodge, 2005.

Cottages

Brunskill, R.W. *Houses and Cottages of Britain*. Gollancz, 1997.

Clifton-Taylor, Alec. *The Pattern of English Building*. Faber and Faber, 1972.

Mason, Peter F. *Hampshire – a sense of place*. Hampshire Books, 1994.

Penoyre, John and Penoyre, Jane. *Houses in the Landscape*. Faber and Faber, 1978.

Ward, Colin. *Cotters and Squatters, housing's hidden history*. Five Leaves Publications, 2002.

Wordsworth, William. *Guide to the Lakes*. 1810.

Counties

Davies, N. *The Isles: a History*. Papermac, 2000.

Denton, P. (Ed). *Betjeman's London*. John Murray, 1988.

Association of British Counties website: www.abcounties.co.uk

Dawn Chorus

Greenoak, F. *All the Birds of the Air: The names, lore and literature of British Birds*. Andre Deutsch, 1979.

Nicholson E.M. and Koch, L. *Songs of Wild Birds*. Witherby, 1936.

Dog Roses

Grigson, Geoffrey. *The Englishman's Flora*. Paladin, 1975.

Keble Martin, W. *The Concise British Flora in Colour*. Ebury Press and Michael Joseph, 1965.

Vickery, Roy. *A Dictionary of Plant Lore*. OUP, 1995.

Dragons

Crossley-Holland, Kevin. *British Folk Tales*. Orchard Books, 1987.

Farmer, David Hugh. *The Oxford Dictionary of Saints*. OUP, 1978/1987.

Field, John. *A History of English Field Names*. Longman, 1993.

Heaney, Seamus. *Beowulf*. Faber and Faber, 1999.

Simpson, Jacqueline. *British Dragons*. Batsford, 1980.

Westwood, Jennifer. *Albion*. Paladin, 1987.

Drove Roads

Addison, Sir William. *The Old Roads of England*. Batsford, 1980.

Belsey, Valerie. *Discovering Green Lanes*. Green Books, 2001.

Raistrick, Arthur. *The Pennine Dales*. Arrow 1968/72.

Taylor, Christopher. *Roads and Tracks of Britain*. J.M. Dent, 1979.

Toulson, Shirley. *The Drovers*. Shire, 1980.

Drystone Walls

Brooks, Alan, Adcock, Sean, Agate, Elizabeth. *Dry Stone Walling*. BTCV, 2003.

Hoskins, W.G. *The Making of the English Landscape*. Hodder and Stoughton, 1955.

Hoskins, W.G. *One Man's England*. BBC, 1978.

Earthworks

Cavendish, Richard. Prehistoric England. Artus Books, 1983/1993.

Glanville, Roger. In *Holding Your Ground*, Angela King & Sue Clifford. Maurice Temple Smith, 1985.

English Heritage.

Exmoor Ponies

Exmoor Pony Society.

Farms & Farmsteads

Brunskill, R.W. *Traditional Farm Buildings of Britain*. Victor Gollancz, 1999.

Massingham, H.J. *English Downland*. Batsford, 1936.

Mercer, Eric. *English Vernacular Houses*. RCHM HMSO, 1975/9.

English Heritage.

Ferries

Wheatley, Keith. *National Maritime Museum Guide to Maritime Britain*. Webb and Bower, 1990.

Field Patterns

Hall, David. 'Turning the Plough' in *Midland Open Fields: landscape character and proposals for management*. English Heritage and Northamptonshire County Council, 2001.

King, Angela and Clifford, Sue. *Field Days: a poetry anthology*. Green Books, 1998.

Taylor, Christopher. *Fields in the English Landscape*. Alan Sutton, 1987.

Tindall, Gillian. *The Fields Beneath*. Granada, 1981.

A Manifesto for Fields and Field Days. Common Ground, 1997.

Footbridges

De Mare, Eric. *The Bridges of Britain*. Batsford, 1954.

Highways Agency. *The Appearance of Bridges and other Highway Structures*. HMSO, 1996.

Jervois, E. *The Ancient Bridges of Mid and Eastern England*. Architectural Press, 1932.

Footpaths

Hannigan, Des. *Ancient Trackways*. Pavilion, 1994.

MacColl, Ewan. 'The Manchester Rambler'. 1932.

Taplin, Kim. *The English Path*. The Boydell Press, 1979.

Gates

Moreland, T.E. 'The Field Gates of England'. *The Countryman*, Summer 1961.

Tanner, Robin and Tanner, Heather. *Wiltshire Village*, Robin Garton, 1939/1978.

Wright, Joseph. *The English Dialect Dictionary*. 1898.

Glow-worms

Robinson, Eric and Summerfield, Geoffrey. *John Clare Selected Poems and Prose*. OUP, 1978.

Tyler, John. *The Glow-worm*. Lakeside Printing, 2002.

Green Lanes

Belsey, Valerie. *The Green Lanes of England*. Green Books, 1998.

Hippisley Cox, R. *The Green Roads of England*. Methuen, 1914.

Wainwright, Alfred. *A Bowland Sketchbook*. Michael Joseph, 1991.

Greetings

Rawling, Tom. 'The Old Showfield' in *Field Days* (King, Angela and Clifford, Sue, Eds). Green Books, 1998.

Trudgill, Peter. *The Dialects of England*. Basil Blackwell, 1990.

Hares

Auden, W.H. and Isherwood, Christopher. *Dog Beneath the Skin*. Faber and Faber, 1935.

Blake, William. *Auguries of Innocence*. 1789.

Buczacki, Stefan. *Fauna Britannica*. Hamlyn, 2002.

Ewart Evans, George and Thomson, David. *The Leaping Hare*. Faber and Faber, 1972.

Hedges

Blunden, Edmund. 'The Landscape' in *The Legacy of England*. Batsford, 1935.

Brooks, Alan and Agate, Elizabeth. *Hedging: A Practical Handbook* . BTCV, 1998.

Nicolson, Adam. 'Hedging the prospects for the Millennium'. *Sunday Telegraph*, 9 April 1995.

Williamson, Tom. *Hedges and Walls*. National Trust, 2002.

Hills

Gelling, Margaret and Cole, Ann. *The Landscape of Place-Names*. Shaun Tyas, 2000.

Housman A.E. *A Shropshire Lad*.

Ice Skating

Bray, William (Ed). *The Diary of John Evelyn*. 1818.

Griffin, A. Harry. 'Country Diary'. *Guardian*, 14 January 2002; 21 April 2003 and 15 December 2003.

Leapman, Michael. *London's River: A History of The Thames*. Pavilion Books, 1991.

Legg, Rodney. *The Stour Valley: From Stourhead to Christchurch*. Halsgrove, 2003.

Inns

Ashley, Peter. *Pubs and inns – Local heroes*. Everyman/ English Heritage, 2001.

Burke, John. *The English Inn*. Batsford, 1981.

Burke, Thomas. *The English Inn*. Herbert Jenkins, 1947.

Jack and Jill

Green, Madalyn. *The Rhyme of Banbury Cross*. Banbury Museum, nd.

Harrowven, Jean. *The Origins of Rhymes, Songs and Sayings*. Pryor Publications, 1998.

Opie, Iona and Opie, Peter (Eds). *The Oxford Dictionary of Nursery Rhymes*. OUP, 1997.

Kerbstones

Clifton-Taylor, Alec and Ireson, A.S. *English Stone Building*. Gollancz, 1983/1994.

Joyce, Barry et al. *Derbyshire Detail and Character*. Alan Sutton, 1996.

Robinson, Eric. *London Illustrated Geological Walks, Book Two*. Scottish Academic Press, 1985.

Robinson, Eric. 'The Stones of the Mile End Road: A geology of Middlemiss country'. *Proceedings of the Geologists' Association, 108*, 1997.

Landmark Trees

Mabey, Richard. *Flora Britannica*. Chatto and Windus, 1996.

Stukeley, William. *Antonine Itineraries*. 1723.

Wilks, J.H. *Trees of the British Isles in History and Legend*. Frederick Muller, 1972.

Letterboxing

Swinscow, Anne. *Dartmoor Letterboxes*. Kirkford Publications, 1984.

Manhole Covers

Aaron, Henry. *Street Furniture*. Shire, 1980.

Ashley, Peter. *Hard Furnishings*. English Heritage/Everyman, 2002.

Moon

Field, John. *English Field Names*. David and Charles, 1972.

Grigson, Geoffrey. *The Englishman's Flora*. Paladin, 1975.

Hough, Carole and Cox, Barrie. 'Moonhill.' *Journal of the English Place-Names Society*, 28, 1995/6.

Oswald, Alice. *The Thing in the Gap-Stone Stile*. Oxford Poets, 1996.

Nomansland

OS Map Explorer OL30 at 940075.

Orchards

'Orchards and Wildlife' (conference papers). Common Ground/English Nature, 1999.

The Common Ground Book of Orchards. Common Ground, 2000.

Parks

Girouard, Mark. *The English Town*. Yale University Press, 1990.

Greenhalgh, Liz and Worpole, Ken. *Park Life: Urban Parks and Social Renewal*. Comedia and Demos, 1995.

Promenades

Somerville, Christopher. *Britain Beside the Sea*. Grafton Books, 1989.

Shifting Sands, Design and the Changing Image of English Seaside Towns. English Heritage and CABE, 2003.

Quarters

Cattell, John and Hawkins, Bob. *The Birmingham Jewellery Quarter*. English Heritage, 2000.

Sheffield City Centre Strategy. Sheffield City Council, 1994.

Rivers

Clifford, Sue. 'The Ducks Swim in Stone' in *River Calling*. London Rivers Association, 2002.

Hole, Christina. *English Folklore*. Batsford, 1940/1945.

Milton, John. 'Rivers arise; whether thou be the Son' in *The River's Voice* (King,

Angela and Clifford, Sue, Eds). Green Books, 2000.

Ruskin, John. *The Elements of Drawing*. Smith, Elder, 1857/ 1973.

Rivers, Rhynes and Running Brooks. Common Ground, 2000.

Rocks

Beckensall, Stan. *Northumberland, The Power of Place*. Tempus, 2001.

Munby, Lionel M. *The Hertfordshire Landscape*. Hodder and Stoughton, 1977.

Rogers, Frank. *Curiosities of Derbyshire*. Derbyshire Countryside, 2000.

Rookeries

Cocker, Mark and Mabey, Richard. Birds Britannica. Chatto & Windus, 2005.

Jefferies, Richard. *Field and Farm*. Phoenix House, 1957.

Sculptures

Randall-Page, Peter et al. *Granite Song, A Common Ground Project*. Devon Books, 1999.

Plymouth Waterfront Walk. Plymouth City Council, 2001.

Sheep

Hartley, Dorothy. *The Land of England*. Macdonald and Jane's Publishers, 1979.

Wallace, Robert. *Farm Live Stock of Great Britain*. Oliver and Boyd, 1907.

Stepping-Stones

Grigson, Geoffrey. *Geoffrey Grigson's Countryside*. Ebury Press, 1982.

Stiles

Lovett Jones, Gareth. *English Country Lanes*. Wildwood House, 1988.

Roberts, Michael. *Gates and Stiles*. Old Cockerel Press, 2001.

Robinson, Eric and Summerfield, Geoffrey(Eds*). The Selected Poems and Prose of John Clare*. OUP, 1978.

Swimming Places

Deakin, Roger. *Waterlog*. Chatto and Windus, 1999.

Wordsworth, William. *Selections from Wordsworth*. Ginn and Co Ltd, 1932/1958.

Terriers

Croxton Smith, A. *British Dogs*. Collins, 1945.

Fogle, Dr Bruce. *The Encyclopaedia of the Dog*. Dorling Kindersley, 1995.

Hancock, David. *Old Working Dogs*. Shire, 1998.

Heath, Veronica. 'Brave Hearts' (Country Diary). *Guardian*, 9 November 2001.

Plummer, D. Brian. *The Sporting Terrier*. The Boydell Press, 1992.

Verges

Martin, Stephen. *The Long Meadow: an historical ecology of roadsides in Britain*. Landscapes, 2003.

Villages

Darley, Gillian. *Villages of Vision*. Paladin, 1978.

Massingham, H.J. *English Downland* Batsford, 1936.

Sharpe, Thomas. *The Anatomy of the Village*. Penguin, 1946.

Taylor, Christopher. *Village and Farmstead*. George Philip, 1984.

Wood, Eric S. *Historical Britain*. Harvill Press, 1995.

Wayside & Boundary Crosses

Beadle, J. Brian. *Walking to Crosses on the North York Moors*. Trailblazer Publishing, 1998.

Harrison, Bill. *Dartmoor Stone Crosses*. Devon Books, 2001.

Langdon, Andrew. *Stone Crosses in North Cornwall*. The Federation of Old Cornwall Societies, 1992/Andrew Langdon, 1996.

Ogilvie, Elizabeth and Sleightholme, Audrey. *The Illustrated Guide to the Crosses on the North York Moors*. The Village Green Press, 1994.

Rowe, Laura. *Granite Crosses of West Cornwall*. Bradford Barton, 1973.

Wildflowers

King, Angela. *Paradise Lost?* Friends of the Earth, 1980.

Mabey, Richard. *Flora Britannica*. Chatto and Windus, 1996.

Perring, F.H. and Walters, S.M. *Atlas of the British Flora*. Botanical Society of the British Isles, 1990.

Vickery, Roy. *A Dictionary of Plant Lore*. OUP, 1995.

Woods

Marren, Peter. *Woodland Heritage*. David and Charles, 1990.

Rackham, Oliver. *Ancient Woodland, its history, vegetation and uses in England*. Castlepoint Press, 2003.

Ratcliffe, D.A. (Ed). *A Nature Conservation Review*. Cambridge University Press, 1977.

Xanadu

Clayre, Alasdair (Ed). *Nature and Industrialization*. Open University, 1977.

Coleridge, Samuel Taylor. 'In Xanadu'. 1797 (poem from the Crewe Manuscript, British Museum).

Holmes, Richard. *Coleridge: Early Visions*. Hodder and Stoughton, 1989.

Zigzags

Lindley, Kenneth. *Seaside Architecture*. Hugh Evelyn, 1973.

Mabey, Richard. 'Introduction' to *Gilbert White, The Natural History of Selborne*. Penguin, 1977.

The Illustrators:

Clifford Harper, *Alleys*, page 1; *Churches*, page 21, 22; *Hills*, page 85

David Holmes, *Ancient Trees*, page 5; *Footpaths*, page 65; *Rocks*, pages 112, 113

Lucinda Rogers, *Bells & Bell-Ringing*, page 13; *Cottages*, page 34; *Gates*, page 69

Nick Hardcastle, *Bluebells*, page 16; *Footbridges*, page 64

Glyn Goodwin, *Cairns*, page 18; *Drystone Walls*, page 48; *Wayside & Boundary Crosses*, page 135

Chloë Cheese, *Canals*, page 20; *Jack and Jill*, page 91

Mickey Georgeson, *Cornish Pasties*, page 32

David Atkinson, *Counties*, page 37

Mark Greenwood, *Dragons*, page 44

David Inshaw, *Earthworks*, page 51

Ken Cox, *Farms & Farmsteads*, page 55, 56

Mary Roberts-Hogan, *Ferries*, pages 58, 59

Graham Bence, *Field Patterns*, page 60

Peter Ursem, *Footbridges*, page 63

Antony Gormley, *Footpaths*, page 67; *Sculptures*, page 117

Richard Allen, *Gates*, page 70; *Rookeries*, page 115; *Sheep*, page 121; *Stiles*, page 125

Francis Mosley, *Green Lanes*, page 73; *Manhole Covers*, page 98, 99

Stephen Turner, *Hares*, page 77

Toby Holmes, *Hedges*, page 80 (after Linda Francis, from *Hedging: A Practical Handbook*, BTCV, 1998); Jack and Jill page 90 (From photograph by Angela King).

David Gentleman, *Inns*, page 89

Robert Maude, *Landmark Trees*, page 95

Stuart Newman, *Letterboxing*, page 97

Peter Blake, *Moon*, page 100

Colin Kennedy, *Orchards*, page 103

Ivan Allen, *Promenades*, page 107

Darren Giddings, *Rivers*, page 110

Ian Pollock, *Rookeries*, page 116

Andrew Davidson, *Terriers*, page 129

Matthew Dennis, *Wildflowers*, page 137

Selected quotes by permission of:

Readers Union for John and Jane Penoyre, *Houses in the Landscape: a Regional Study of Vernacular Building Styles in England and Wales*, 1978; Hodder & Stoughton Ltd for W.G. Hoskins, *The Making of the English Landscape*, 1955 and 2005; Chrysalis Books Group plc for Edmund Blunden, *The Landscape in the legacy of England*, ©Edmund Blunden, 1935; H.J. Massingham, English Downland, © H.J.Massingham, 1936; Caroline Grigson, Literary Executor of the estate of the late Geoffrey Grigson.

Our sincere apologies if we have missed or misrepresented anyone. Please inform us so that we can rectify this.

Acknowledgements

Very many thanks to everyone who contacted us with information about their locality and passions as well as individuals, groups, societies, organisations, publishers, agents, executors and trustees for their generosity. A comprehensive list of thanks and credits is to be found in the full Bibliography and Acknowledgements in *England in Particular*.

Common Ground is a small charity dependent upon grants and donations. We offer most grateful thanks to our funders 1985–2006 including Defra Environmental Action Fund, Carnegie UK Trust, Cobb Trust, John Ellerman Foundation, Garfield Weston Foundation, Headley Trust, Lyndhurst Settlement, Raphael Trust, Tedworth Trust, Countryside Agency, English Nature, National Lottery Arts Council of England, Esmée Fairbairn Charitable Trust, and many more.

Particular thanks to Darren Giddings, Kate O'Farrell, Gail Vines, who helped us research and draft the book and to Katrina Porteous, our Northumberland and literature correspondent; David Holmes, Toby and Polly who oversaw all of the illustrative work; all of our illustrators who responded to our demands for particularity; our trustees and friends: Barbara Bender, Roger Deakin, Robin Grove-White, Richard Mabey, Rupert Nabarro, Fraser Harrison, Robert Hutchison; our agent Vivien Green at Shiel Land; our original mentors at Hodder & Stoughton: Richard Atkinson (especially), Elizabeth Hallett, Nicola Docherty, Simon Shelmerdine, Karen Geary, Rachael Oakden, Hilary Bird, Barbara Roby; designers Stuart Smith, Karl Shanahan, Victoria Forrest.

And in 2013/14 – at John Murray Press Nick Davies MD; at Saltyard Books warm thanks to Elizabeth Hallett – publisher, Kate Miles, Christine Gilland, Lyndsey Ng; designer Clare Skeats and cover illustrator Joe McLaren.

England in Particular was first published in Great Britain in 2006 by Hodder & Stoughton

Journeys Through England in Particular: On Foot was first published in Great Britain in 2014 by Saltyard Books
An imprint of Hodder & Stoughton
An Hachette UK company

Common Ground is a charity (no.326335) and has been grateful for grant support from the Cobb Trust, Countryside Agency, Defra Environmental Action Fund, the John Ellerman Foundation, the Garfield Weston Foundation, the Headley Trust, the Tedworth Charitable Trust, the Lyndhurst Settlement, and many others.

I

A CIP catalogue record for this title is available from the British Library.

ISBN 978 1 444 78961 4
eBook ISBN 978 1 444 78962 1

Book design by Clare Skeats
Typeset in Portrait Text and Gill Sans

Printed and bound in China by C&C Offset Printing Co., Ltd

Hodder & Stoughton policy is to use papers that are natural, renewable and recyclable products and made from wood grown in sustainable forests. The logging and manufacturing processes are expected to conform to the environmental regulations of the country of origin.

Saltyard Books
338 Euston Road
London NW1 3BH

www.saltyardbooks.co.uk

BRING THE COUNTRYSIDE *to the* **TOWN.**
Keep the fruit, vegetable and local produce **markets** open and alive. We should be able to buy **NORFOLK BIFFINS** in Norwich and **LAXTON'S SUPERB** in Bedford.

PLACES CARRY MEANING
in their associations and symbolisms. *Don't plough through significance, it cannot be re-created.* The well or tree may be the reason why a place is where it is.

LET NATURE IN.
Encourage the plants that want to grow in your locality. You'll find a succession of GOOD *and* DIVERSE neighbours that bring **RICHNESS TO YOUR DOORSTEP.**

NAMES CARRY **RESONANCES** AND SECRETS. **RESPECT LOCAL NAMES** *and add new ones with* **CARE.**
It is not good enough to call a new estate 'Badger's Mead' when the badgers have been **DESTROYED.**

CHAMPION THE **ORDINARY** *and the* **EVERYDAY.**

GET TO **KNOW** YOUR PLACE **INTIMATELY.**
Search out **PARTICULARITY** AND **PATINA,** *add new* **LAYERS OF INTEREST.**

QUALITY CANNOT BE **QUANTIFIED.**
You know when something is important to you – make SUBJECTIVE AND *EMOTIONAL* ARGUMENTS. Don't be put off because professionals have marginalised all the things they can't count. **MAKE THEM LISTEN** *and* LOOK.

Remember the depth of PEOPLE'S ATTACHMENT TO **PLACES.**
Do not undermine **LOCAL PRIDE** and rootedness with insensitive change.

REVEAL THE GEOLOGY.
Use the brick and stone of the locality. *Reinforce the colour, patterns, texture,* **CRAFTSMANSHIP** *and work of the place.*